THE HIDDEN TREASURES IN THE GOSPELS

Jesus
Our Savior and Friend

AN INDUCTIVE BIBLE STUDY BY **EVELYN WHEELER**

P.O. Box 23537, Richfield, MN 55423

Scripture verses in this book are taken from the New American Standard Bible ®, Copyright © 1960, 1962, 1963, 1968, 1971, 1972, 1973, 1975, 1977, 1995 by the Lockman Foundation. Used by permission.

Truth Trackers: The Hidden Treasures in the Gospels: Jesus Our Savior and Friend
Copyright © 2005 by Evelyn Wheeler
Published by Liberty Books
P.O. Box 23537
Richfield, Minnesota 55423

Cover design by Alpha Advertising

Library of Congress Cataloging-in-Publication Data
(Provided by Cassidy Cataloguing Services, Inc.)

Wheeler, Evelyn.

   Jesus, our savior and friend : the hidden treasures in the gospels : an inductive Bible study / by Evelyn Wheeler. — 1st ed. — Richfield, MN : Liberty Books, 2005.

     p. ; cm. (Hidden treasures)
     Audience: ages 8-12. "Truth trackers." ISBN: 1-886930-26-0

     1. Jesus Christ—Biography—Juvenile literature. 2. Bible stories, English—N.T.—Gospels. 3. Bible—Children's use. 4. [Bible—Selections]. I. Title.

BT302 .W44 2005
232.9/01—dc22   0501

All rights reserved. No part of this book may be reproduced in any form or by any means without written permission from the publisher.

Printed in the United States of America.

05 06 07 08 09 10 11 12 / 10 9 8 7 6 5 4 3 2 1

Contents

    Introduction: The Hidden Treasures of the Bible 5
1. Our Adventure Begins! 7
2. Who Is This Jesus? 21
3. The Start of Something Big! 35
4. How to Become a Follower 53
5. The Puzzle of Parables 69
6. Tracking Truth in Parables 85
7. Jesus the Miracle Worker 99
8. Miracles, Miracles, More Miracles! 113
9. What's in a Name? 131
10. The Beginning of the End 143
11. The Famous Trial of Jesus 159
12. The Greatest Victory of All 171
    Treasure Map 187
    Timeline of the Life of Christ 191
    Key to Games 193

Hidden Treasures of the Bible

Welcome to a study of the life of Jesus Christ. You're joining a great group of kids called Truth Trackers who are always digging in search of the truth of the Word of God!

Our study is like a great archaeological dig! Archaeologists are people who dig through the remains of old civilizations to understand how men, women, and children lived thousands of years ago. As they piece together bits of the past that they unearth, they eventually get a bigger picture of what life was like.

Like archaeologists, we are going to dig into the Bible to see what we can discover about the life of Christ. Below the surface of the verses we will dig through, you will discover many truths and treasures. Together we're going to dig and sift and sort through these Bible verses so that you can come away with truths that will help you for the rest of your life. Yes, the great thing about the dig is you'll get a bigger picture too—a picture of what God is saying to you about some important issues for life.

Before you start, meet a friendly camel named Clayton. His ancestors lived in Bible times, so he has heard all of the stories of the Bible as they have been passed down from generation to generation. He even had a distant uncle in Bethlehem the night Jesus was born! Clayton will be the head archaeologist on this exciting adventure! He'll talk you through each dig.

As you begin this incredible dig on the life of Jesus, remember that archaeologists work very long, hard hours. They have exciting jobs, and the result of their work is very rewarding, but it is not easy work! Remember, too, that you can't unearth the treasures that are to be found in the Bible without lots of work!

You won't discover the kind of truths we are after by sitting in front of the television or staring at your computer. You must get up, grab your boots, hat, tools, and dig into the Word. You have to push through all five layers of each dig to understand what God wants to say to you. It won't happen if you don't get up, dig in, and do your part.

There will be many, many times throughout your life that you'll be glad you spent this time digging in the Bible because you'll know what God says and what He wants. And then you'll be able to do the right thing and please Him! At the end of our 12 digs, you'll have a treasure chest full of truth that will help you the rest of your life.

We're almost ready to get started digging. First, let me tell you some "rules of the road":

Tools of the Trade: At the beginning of each lesson is a list of tools you'll need in order to complete the lesson. You should always gather these together before you begin the work. Like a good archaeologist, you need the right tools to get the job done.

Directions for Diggers: This short section is the introduction to each dig and gives you an idea of the dig's topic. Remember that on any dig there is a head archaeologist who directs the dig, so Clayton will talk you through this section.

Chart the Course: You'll have a chance to work on maps and charts that will help you understand the material. At a dig site, there is a graph or map that shows the team where to dig. These maps and charts in your study will point the way to truth treasures for you! Whenever you see a map, be sure you look at it to find the locations mentioned in the work you're doing that day.

Clues: As you work through the digs, from time to time you'll be given clues that will help you unearth truth. Every site has clues that point to where special treasures can be discovered. You'll be given clues to point you to truth as you work.

Treasure Map: It is easier to find treasures if you have a master map of the area where you're working. The verses on the life of Christ will be your master map for this dig. It is called the "Treasure Map" because through the study of these passages, you'll discover GREAT treasures. These sections of Scripture, or passages, are printed at the back of your study book on pages 187-190.

Checking in with Headquarters: Each time you begin a new dig, you should pray and ask the Holy Spirit to teach you truth. Just like on a dig when everyone checks in with the head guy for directions for the day, you should check in for help with your study.

Special Find: On digs, there are times when very special artifacts are uncovered. In fact, Clayton was on a dig the other day when a water jug was unearthed—and it was all in one piece! This is a very special find because most of the time, bits and pieces of treasure are pulled out and have to be pieced together later. These sections will help you find very special treasures.

Truth Treasures for the Week: At the end of each week's dig, you'll see a place to record three truth treasures you discovered. On an archaeological dig, when a section of the dig is complete, all of the finds are tagged and information about each is noted. In the same way, you'll tag some key truths and note them. Be sure not to skip this section! You're on your own when it comes to this part, but it is very important!

Bury the Treasure: One of the wisest things you can do is to memorize the Word of God. Each dig has a special treasure that you'll unearth, and you'll want to bury it in your heart.

Puzzles: Throughout the study, you'll find a variety of fun puzzles that will help you review the truth you're learning. It is like being on a dig and watching as the head archaeologist tries to put broken pieces together to see if they have discovered a table, a jar, a bowl, or who knows what! It'll be fun to work through these and see what you discover! (A key to each puzzle can be found at the back of the book so that you can check your answers.)

**Well, you're prepared. Are you ready?
I hope so. Take off to Dig One. Clayton will meet you there.**

Dig 1

Our Adventure Begins!

Tools of the Trade

1. Colored pencils
2. Pen or pencil
3. Treasure Map of the sections from the gospels on pages 187-190
4. Encounters with Jesus on page 18-19
5. Chart: A Look At the Birth of Christ on page 17
6. Maze to the Manger on page 20
7. Timeline of the Life of Christ on pages 191-192

Directions for Diggers

Have you ever heard people talk about Jesus and wondered why He was so special? You may know what your parents think about Him. And you may have heard your pastor or other adults talk about how powerful He is, how holy He was, or how He is even equal with God. But do you ever think about what they mean when they talk like this? And if you do think about it, do you understand why they think like they do?

I hope you have wondered. I hope you have tried to figure out what is so special about this Man who claimed to be God. I know that this study we are going to do together will answer many of your questions. It will help you to understand who Jesus is, where He is today, and what He did, and is doing—for you personally.

God wants you to know Jesus as well as you know your family or your best friend. In fact, He wants you to know Jesus even better! And He wants you to realize that Jesus knows you. That He cares about you. That He is interested in everything you do, think, and say. That He will always be with you. That He is around when you need Him. That you can trust Him and tell Him anything.

So let's get started in our study. You'll see that studying the Bible can be a lot of fun. It may seem like a lot of work sometimes too, but don't give up. Ask God to help you to be the best student you can be.

And here is a clue to help you get off to a great start: **Clue #1:** It will be much easier if you work on each dig one layer at a time. Just dig through one layer each day instead of trying to work through an entire dig in one sitting.

LAYER ONE: Checking in with Headquarters

1. Sometimes when we read the Word of God, it can be hard to understand all that it is saying. It can be difficult to see what the Word of God means for us today when it was written so long ago, can't it?

Do you know that you can get extra help to understand the Word of God? Great news, isn't it? Well, in John 16:13, the Bible says, "But when He, the Spirit of truth, comes, He will guide you into all truth..." This verse is a promise to you that the Holy Spirit will help you understand the truth that God has in the Bible!

You can think of it in this way: When you are working on your homework and you don't understand a question that you need to answer, you can ask your mom, dad, brother, or sister for help. Usually someone in your family can help you understand the question and answer it. And if no one knows the answer, they can help you find information that will let you figure out the correct answer. Well, when you pray and ask the Holy Spirit for help, it is like when you ask someone in your family for help. And in the same way that your family helps you find the answer, the Holy Spirit will lead you to the answer, to the truth!

So if you can't understand or figure out what you read in this study or in your Bible, you can pray and ask for help. God wants you to understand! And the good news is that He *always* knows the answer, and He is *never* too busy to listen and help! Sometimes He will show you the answer right away, and sometimes it may take some time for Him to help you see the answer. But He will show you.

Do you remember that we are calling our prayer time for help in understanding the Word of God "checking in with headquarters"?

Our Adventure Begins!

You should check in each day before you begin digging. You wouldn't start on an important archeological dig without checking in with the head archeologists for directions would you? And you don't want to dig into God's Word without asking for the help of the Holy Spirit, your Teacher and Guide.

2. One of the highest man-made places in the world is in Paris, France. It is also one of the most beautiful structures you could ever see. It is the Eiffel Tower. And you can board a large elevator and go to the very top of the tower for a great view of the magnificent city of Paris.

Paris is a large city and has many beautiful bridges and marvelous buildings. When you are on the ground, you can see many of the bridges and numerous buildings. And you can see the beautiful carving on the buildings and get an up-close view of the tremendous size of the lights on the some of the bridges.

But when you go to the top of the Eiffel Tower you can't see the details of the buildings or the size of the lights on the bridges. You get a very different view—a much bigger one. You can look over the entire city and see all of the city at once—all of its bridges and buildings! It is a breathtaking sight.

This week we are going to look at the birth of Christ like we are standing on the top of the Eiffel Tower. We'll focus on the big picture of His birth, not on all of the details. If we took the time to see the details and to try and understand them, it could take us several weeks. And if we spent this kind of time on the details of His birth, we would not have time to look at all of the other parts of His life in the way we want to.

Later as we get further into this study, we will take a close-up look—like when you view the bridges of Paris from the ground—at some of the parables Jesus taught, at some of the miracles He performed, at some of the names He goes by. Because looking at these teachings, miracles, and names will teach you more about who Jesus is and how He wants to work in your life.

But for now, let's go with our big-picture view of the birth of Christ. Are you ready? Your assignment for today is to read the account of the birth of Christ as it is recorded in three of the gospels.

Don't let the length of the reading scare you off. You'll have some help. As you read these passages, ask one of your parents, an older brother or sister, or an older friend to read out loud to you. While they read out loud, you can read silently with them. Reading through these passages at one sitting will help you begin to see all of the accounts of the birth of Jesus Christ—like viewing Paris from the top of the Eiffel Tower lets you see the entire city!

Don't worry if you don't understand some of what you read. Just keep reading. Have you ever heard people say that you climb a mountain one step at a time? Well, in the case of this study, that is a good saying for us to remember. We have a lot of material to cover—material that will reveal the life of Christ to us! So we must take one step at a time to cover all that we want to learn. And the first step is reading these passages pulled together from different books of the Bible that will give you the story of Jesus' birth.

So read the passages on Jesus birth out loud with a family member or friend. This is a part of your Treasure Map that is printed on pages 187-190. But since someone else is helping you read this part, it is also printed below for you. After you finish the entire reading, you're all done for the day!

18Now the birth of Jesus Christ was as follows: when His mother Mary had been betrothed to Joseph, before they came together she was found to be with child by the Holy Spirit. **19**And Joseph her husband, being a righteous man and not wanting to disgrace her, planned to send her away secretly. **20**But when he had considered this, behold, an angel of the Lord appeared to him in a dream, saying, "Joseph, son of David, do not be afraid to take Mary as your wife; for the Child who has been conceived in her is of the Holy Spirit. **21**"She will bear a Son; and you shall call His name Jesus, for He will save His people from their sins." **22**Now all this took place to fulfill what was spoken by the Lord through the prophet: **23**"BEHOLD, THE VIRGIN SHALL BE WITH CHILD AND SHALL BEAR A SON, AND THEY SHALL CALL HIS NAME IMMANUEL," which translated means, "GOD WITH US."(Matthew 1:18-23)

26Now in the sixth month the angel Gabriel was sent from God to a city in Galilee called Nazareth, **27**to a virgin engaged to a man whose name was Joseph, of the descendants of David; and the virgin's name was Mary. **28**And coming in, he said to her, "Greetings, favored one! The Lord *is* with you." **29**But she was very perplexed at *this* statement, and kept pondering what kind of salutation this was. **30**The angel said to her, "Do not be afraid, Mary; for you have found favor with God. **31**"And behold, you will conceive in your womb and bear a son, and you shall name Him Jesus. **32**"He will be great and will be called the Son of the Most High; and the Lord God will give Him the throne of His father David; **33**and He will reign over the house of Jacob forever, and His kingdom will have no end." **34**Mary said to the angel, "How can this be, since I am a virgin?" **35**The angel answered and said to her, "The Holy Spirit will come upon you, and the power of the Most High will overshadow you; and for that reason the holy Child shall be called the Son of God." (Luke 1:26-35)

1Now it came about in those days that a decree went out from Caesar Augustus, that a census be taken of all the inhabited earth. **2**This was the first census taken while Quirinius was governor of Syria. **3**And all were proceeding to register for the census, everyone to his own city. **4**And Joseph also went up from Galilee, from the city of Nazareth, to Judea, to the city of David, which is called Bethlehem, because he was of the house and family of David, **5**in order to register along with Mary, who was engaged to him, and was with child. **6**And it came about that while they were there, the days were completed for her to give birth. **7**And she gave birth to her first-born

Our Adventure Begins!

son; and she wrapped Him in cloths, and laid Him in a manger, because there was no room for them in the inn. **8**And in the same region there were *some* shepherds staying out in the fields, and keeping watch over their flock by night. **9**And an angel of the Lord suddenly stood before them, and the glory of the Lord shone around them; and they were terribly frightened. **10**And the angel said to them, "Do not be afraid; for behold, I bring you good news of a great joy which shall be for all the people; **11**for today in the city of David there has been born for you a Savior, who is Christ the Lord. **12**"And this *will be* a sign for you: you will find a baby wrapped in cloths, and lying in a manger." **13**And suddenly there appeared with the angel a multitude of the heavenly host praising God, and saying,

14"Glory to God in the highest,
And on earth peace among men with whom He is pleased."

15And it came about when the angels had gone away from them into heaven, that the shepherds *began* saying to one another, "Let us go straight to Bethlehem then, and see this thing that has happened which the Lord has made known to us." **16**And they came in haste and found their way to Mary and Joseph, and the baby as He lay in the manger. **17**And when they had seen this, they made known the statement which had been told them about this Child. **18**And all who heard it wondered at the things which were told them by the shepherds. **19**But Mary treasured up all these things, pondering them in her heart. **20**And the shepherds went back, glorifying and praising God for all that they had heard and seen, just as had been told them. **21**And when eight days were completed before His circumcision, His name was *then* called Jesus, the name given by the angel before He was conceived in the womb. **22**And when the days for their purification according to the law of Moses were completed, they brought Him up to Jerusalem to present Him to the Lord **23**(as it is written in the Law of the Lord, "EVERY FIRST-BORN MALE THAT OPENS THE WOMB SHALL BE CALLED HOLY TO THE LORD"), **24**and to offer a sacrifice according to what was said in the Law of the Lord, "A PAIR OF TURTLEDOVES, OR TWO YOUNG PIGEONS." **25**And behold, there was a man in Jerusalem whose name was Simeon; and this man was righteous and devout, looking for the consolation of Israel; and the Holy Spirit was upon him. **26**And it had been revealed to him by the Holy Spirit that he would not see death before he had seen the Lord's Christ. **27**And he came in the Spirit into the temple; and when the parents brought in the child Jesus, to carry out for Him the custom of the Law, **28**then he took Him into his arms, and blessed God, and said,

29"Now Lord, Thou dost let Thy bond-servant depart
In peace, according to Thy word;
30For my eyes have seen Thy salvation,
31Which Thou hast prepared in the presence of all peoples,
32A LIGHT OF REVELATION TO THE GENTILES,
And the glory of Thy people Israel."

33And His father and mother were amazed at the things which were being said about Him. **34**And Simeon blessed them, and said to Mary His mother, "Behold, this *Child* is appointed for the fall and rise of many in Israel, and for a sign to be opposed— **35**and a sword will pierce even your own soul—to the end that thoughts from many hearts may be revealed." **36**And there was a prophetess, Anna the daughter of Phanuel, of the tribe of Asher. She was advanced in years, having lived with a husband seven years after her marriage, **37**and then as a widow to the age of eighty-four. And she never left the temple, serving night and day with fastings and prayers. **38**And at that very moment she came up and *began* giving thanks to God, and continued to speak of Him to all those who were looking for the redemption of Jerusalem. **39**And when they had performed everything according to the Law of the Lord, they returned to Galilee, to their own city of Nazareth. (Luke 2:1-39)

1In the beginning was the Word, and the Word was with God, and the Word was God. **2**He was in the beginning with God. **3**All things came into being through Him, and apart from Him nothing came into being that has come into being. **4**In Him was life, and the life was the Light of men. **5**The Light shines in the darkness, and the darkness did not comprehend it. **6**There came a man sent from God, whose name was John. **7**He came as a witness, to testify about the Light, so that all might believe through him. **8**He was not the Light, but *he came* to testify about the Light. **9**There was the true Light which, coming into the world, enlightens every man. **10**He was in the world, and the world was made through Him, and the world did not know Him. **11**He came to His own, and those who were His own did not receive Him. **12**But as many as received Him, to them He gave the right to become children of God, *even* to those who believe in His name, **13**who were born, not of blood nor of the will of the flesh nor of the will of man, but of God. **14**And the Word became flesh, and dwelt among us, and we saw His glory, glory as of the only begotten from the Father, full of grace and truth. **15**John testified˙ about Him and cried out, saying, "This was He of whom I said, 'He who comes after me has a higher rank than I, for He existed before me.'" **16**For of His fullness we have all received, and grace upon grace. **17**For the Law was given through Moses; grace and truth were realized through Jesus Christ. (John 1:1-17)

I am very proud of you for wanting to work through this study! I am excited about what I know you will learn. I'll look forward to seeing you when you begin digging into Layer Two!

LAYER TWO: The Big Picture

Yesterday you read through the passages from three of the gospels that tell us about the birth of Jesus. You have a good idea of the events that surrounded His coming to earth as a baby!

Now that you have a view of the birth of Christ from atop the Eiffel Tower, let's take the elevator down to the ground, grab our picks, and dig around for a closer look—one passage at a time.

Our Adventure Begins!

1. Now that you will work through the passages on your own, turn to your Treasure Map in the back of the book where the passages from the gospels are printed out for you on pages 187-190 and read through the passage from the Gospel of Matthew. This time you'll be reading it yourself. If you read out loud, you'll remember it better. Today some more of the story from Matthew is added. Be careful just to read the verses from Matthew. Don't keep going when you get to the verses from Luke! Just read the Matthew verses.

2. Now find the chart called "A Look at the Birth of Jesus" at the end of this lesson on page 17. This chart will help you "chart the course." Look at the chart and find the column called "Chapter Titles." In that column are two possible titles for this section from Matthew. Think back over what you read in the passage and circle the title you think is best for the chapter.

Clue #2: Your chapter title should tell you what the author talks about the most in the passage. It should also help you remember what you read.

3. Do you like to draw? I do! Now you get to be an artist! If you don't have your colored pencils, run grab them. You're going to do an illustration.

An illustration is a picture used to explain something. Story books and comic books use lots of illustrations. The artist draws a picture to show your eyes the meaning of the words that you're reading. As you can

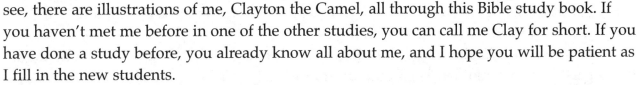

see, there are illustrations of me, Clayton the Camel, all through this Bible study book. If you haven't met me before in one of the other studies, you can call me Clay for short. If you have done a study before, you already know all about me, and I hope you will be patient as I fill in the new students.

It's lots of fun to draw illustrations! Ready? Go back to the chart on page 17. In the column called "Illustrations," beside the title of the passage, draw what you think is the main happening of that passage. You don't have to draw everything that you read about, just draw the main event of the passage. And remember that you are going to do a drawing for the passage from the Gospel of Luke too when you get to Layer Three, so think about the differences in the passages so that your drawings are about what you read in each different passage.

Have fun. I'll see you when we dig into Layer Three!

LAYER THREE: Tracking the Treasure

1. What does a good student of the Bible do before beginning to dig into the truth of the Word of God? If you said "pray," you're right! So take a moment and check in with headquarters. Ask the Holy Spirit to help you understand what God is saying to you in His Word.

Truth Trackers: Jesus Our Savior and Friend

2. Now turn to the Treasure Map at the back of the book and read through the passage on the birth of Christ from the Gospel of Luke beginning on page 188. As you read, remember to think about what this passage tells you that you did not see in the Gospel of Matthew. That will help you to choose a title and draw a great illustration.

3. I want you to be an artist again today. Do exactly what you did yesterday when you worked on the chart at the end of the lesson—only this time, work on the passage from Luke. Decide on your title and draw your illustration.

Enjoy your study time. Catch you tomorrow.

LAYER FOUR: Charting Your Course

Are you enjoying your study? I surely hope so because I am really enjoying having you in the study!

1. Take out your pick again today and dig into the passage from the Gospel of John. I am sure you noticed when you read the passages out loud in Layer One that what you read in this gospel is really different from what you read in Matthew and Luke.

I think the account John records is more poetic in the way it is written. He does not talk about Mary and Joseph. About the manger. About the Wise Men and King Herod. He talks using a part of language we call a metaphor. Have you ever studied this in school? If not, you will. But let me help you a bit with a clue: **Clue #3**: A metaphor is calling something or someone by a name or a term other than its real name.

So you see John talk about Jesus by calling Him something that we do not usually think of one person calling another. See if you can spot what I am talking about as you read the passage from the Gospel of John now. And don't forget to think about the main points of what you read. The Treasure Map has the verses from John beginning on page 190.

2. Do you have your colored pencils? Continue to "chart your course" by choosing your title and by drawing your illustration. Your illustration will be fun because you will need to think a little about it since this section of Scripture is so different from those in Matthew and Luke!

After you finish your work today, take a break from a hot day of digging. Maybe a cool glass of lemonade sounds good. It does to me. See you at the beginning of Layer Five!

LAYER FIVE: Reviewing Your Treasures

1. Today, you'll dig into the treasures you have uncovered in Layers One through Four in an unusual way. Your dig for today is different than any you have done so far because I want you to dig through all that you have learned in this lesson by reviewing in your mind

Our Adventure Begins!

what you have read in the different gospels about the birth of Jesus. **Hint:** It may help you to look at your chart on page 17 where you can see your titles and your illustrations. So think now about what you have learned.

2. Now, go to the drawing Encounters with Jesus on pages 18-19. First, find the town where He was born. Why don't you take one of your colored pencils and circle the name of the town. Now you see where this little town is! Take a few minutes and color this part of the drawing—the area that shows the town where Jesus was born.

3. Now that you have taken a moment to review in your mind and have located the town where Jesus was born, I want you to write your own version of the story of the birth of Christ. Don't look back at the passages! See what you can remember and write your own account as if you were a reporter writing of this amazing birth for your school newspaper or your local hometown paper!

I have left you lots of space on the next page to write, but if your account is shorter than the space I have left, that is fine. Just tell the story as you remember it.

4. Now, ask someone in your family to let you read the story to them! Maybe your family would be your audience after dinner tonight.

5. Before you read your account to someone else, look back at the passages and check for any details you did not remember. Take time to note these at the end of your story or on another sheet of paper so that you have them in your mind and will remember them the next time you have a chance to write the account of Jesus' birth.

6. Before you call it quits for this dig, take a moment for a little fun and see if you can dig through the puzzle called "Maze to the Manger" on page 20.

7. One last thing that will take only one minute! Look at the Timeline of the Life of Christ on pages 191-192. Read page 191 so that you understand the goal of the timeline.

Now, check off the events that you have uncovered in Dig One. You will see a space for you to write the number of the dig beside the event. So when you find the event, just write in One!

You're amazing! You have made it through Dig One, and I am proud of you. You should be proud of yourself too. Mostly, you should be excited that you are learning the Word of God in a new and deeper way. See you at Dig Two. Now take a good break and have some fun!

P.S. Don't forget to "Bury the Treasure," and don't forget to note three truth treasures. If you can't remember what we've talked about earlier on these sections at the end of each lesson, go back to page 6 and review why these two sections are at the end of the lessons.

Truth Trackers: Jesus Our Savior and Friend

TRUTH TREASURES FOR THE WEEK

1.

2.

3.

BURY THE TREASURE:

But as many as received Him, to them He gave the right to become the children of God, *even* to those who believe in His name (John 1:12).

MY ACCOUNT OF THE BIRTH OF JESUS:

Our Adventure Begins!
A Look At the Birth of Jesus

Chapter Titles	Illustrations
Matthew 1:18-2:23	
A Baby Is Born	
Joseph's Dream / The Magis' Visit	
Luke 1:26-35, 2:1-39	
Angel to Mary / The Shepherds' Visit	
Jesus Comes to Earth	
John 1:1-17	
Jesus Came to Earth	
The Word Became Flesh	

Encounters with Jesus

SEA OF GALILEE

SAMARIA

Sychar

NAZARETH

JER

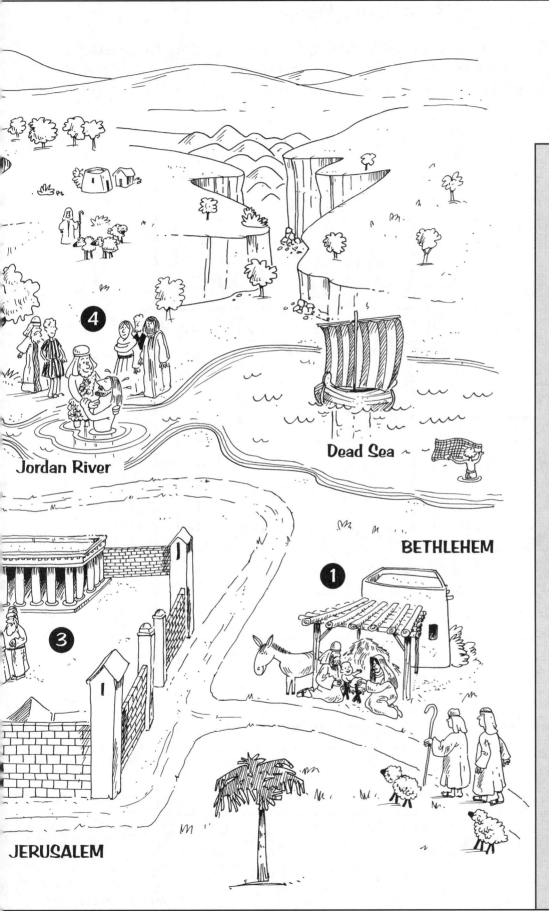

1. You will find a baby in a manger (Luke 2:1-20)

2. Jesus grows up and comes back as a man to talk to His hometown friends (Matthew 4:22-23; Luke 4:16-30)

3. Jesus goes to the Temple at age 12 and returns many times as a man (Luke 2:41-52)

4. Jesus is baptized by His cousin, John (Luke 3:21-23a)

5. Jesus goes to Samaria to meet a woman at a well (John 4:3-30, 40-42)

6. Jesus names the 12 men who He asks to work with Him (Mark 3:13-19)

Truth Trackers

Maze to the Manger

Go on a search for Baby Jesus like the Wise Men did. But watch out for King Herod! He's out to destroy the new King and is looking for Him everywhere. When you find Jesus, worship Him in your heart just like the Wise Men did!

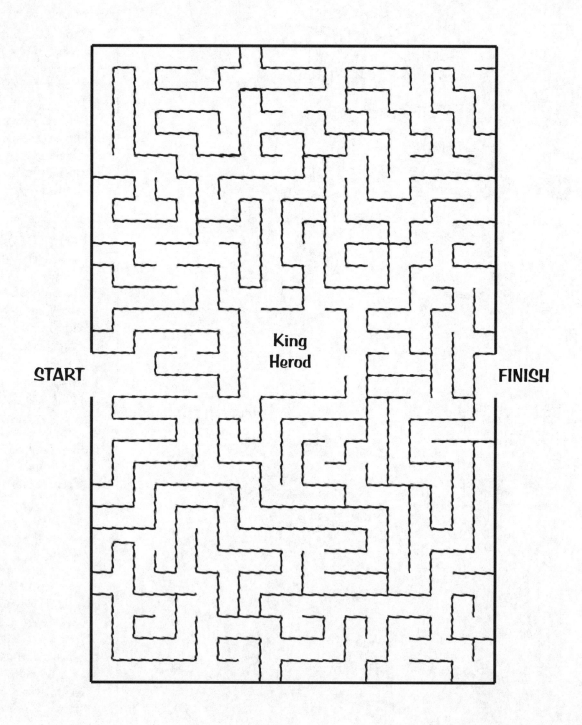

solution on page 193

Dig 2

Who Is This Jesus?

Tools of the Trade

1. Colored pencils
2. Pen or pencil
3. Before and After Jesus Saves You puzzle on page 33

Directions for Diggers

Our dig this week will be awesome! Since in the last dig we looked at the birth of Jesus, in this dig we will see if you can uncover Jesus' identity—who He really is. And you will also unearth the reason Jesus came to earth.

Don't forget the most important thing you can do before you begin to dig into the Word of God—check in with headquarters! Ask the Holy Spirit to help you understand what you will see as you dig into God's Word. Have you checked in yet? If not, stop and pray now.

Okay, ready now? Let's start digging.

LAYER ONE: Do You Know About the Trinity?

Today let's dig all the way through Layer One and discover who Jesus really is.

Truth Trackers: *Jesus Our Savior and Friend*

1. Read John 8:58 and look for the name Jesus calls Himself.

⁵⁸Jesus said to them, "Truly, truly, I say to you, before Abraham was born, I am."

Write here what Jesus calls Himself:

2. Now, let's see if we can discover what this name means and why Jesus would call Himself by this name. Read the first part of Exodus 3:14 and see Who calls Himself "I AM."

¹⁴And God said to Moses, "I AM WHO I AM"…

Who called Himself "I AM" in this verse?

So when Jesus called Himself by the same name that God used to describe Himself, Jesus was saying that He too is God!

3. You may ask how two people can be the same person. It sounds impossible, doesn't it? You may think of twins and think that Jesus using God's name could mean that they are like twins, but it isn't the same. Let's see if we can understand.

First, before we try and understand more about how God and Jesus are the same person, I have one more bit of amazing information for you! The Holy Spirit, who we have been talking about, is also God. So there aren't just two who claim to be God, there are three!

Let's use an illustration or example to help understand what we are talking about.

If you had to explain to someone what ice is, what would you say? You could tell them it is frozen water, couldn't you?

When ice melts in the hot sun and a puddle of water appears, what happens to the puddle? It evaporates! And when the weather conditions are just right, you can even see the water evaporate! Have you ever seen steam? Then, you have seen water in its gaseous state as it evaporates!

Now, you need to think hard with me. When ice is frozen, is it still water? Okay. Now, when the water evaporates and turns into steam, is it still water? The answer to the question is *yes*! So we have seen that one substance—water—can exist in three different forms: water (liquid), ice (solid), and steam (gas).

And if you think of God as one person who exists in three forms, you can better understand that the Bible talks about God who is called the Father, about Jesus who is called the Son, and the Holy Spirit who is called a Spirit. (We can't see the Holy Spirit with our eyes, but the Bible tells us He is in our hearts if we have believed in Jesus and are a Christian!)

4. So, now who would you say Jesus really is?

5. Let's look at another verse that will help you understand the part of God that Jesus is.

¹The beginning of the gospel of Jesus Christ, the Son of God. (Mark 1:1)

When Mark wrote his account of the life of Jesus, he told us in the very first verse who Jesus is. What does Mark call Him?

So, Jesus is the Son of God! He is God, and He came to earth to show us one part of the person of God: the Son of God.

I know that what we have talked about today is a lot to dig through. Even adults have to think very hard to understand how God can be one person and then have three parts all at the same time!

Sometimes, adults use a triangle to illustrate the three parts of God. The triangle is one symbol, but it has three points. So they use the one symbol to show God and each of the three points to represent each part of who He is.

Even if you do not totally understand the idea yet, you at least know about it and can ask God to help you understand.

Take a break! You certainly deserve it. Thanks for all your hard work on this layer! See you at Layer Two soon.

LAYER TWO: A Very Special Mother

Well, the treasure you uncovered in Layer One was a bit of a brain bender, wasn't it? Guess what. Today is another dig that will uncover some awesome treasure, but it is also a dig that will leave you with treasure that you will really have to work to find and grasp.

Today we want to dig through verses that will help you understand how Jesus can be God and be a man at the same time! See, I told you it would take some work to get it!

1. Let's begin by looking at who Jesus' parents were. You actually saw these verses in Dig One when you read about the birth of Jesus, so in a way this exercise will be review for you. But hopefully you will get a closer look this time since you aren't reading so much.

First, let's see again who Jesus' mother was. And let's think about some of the things the angel said to her.

²⁶Now in the sixth month the angel Gabriel was sent from God to a city in Galilee called Nazareth, ²⁷to a virgin engaged to a man whose name was Joseph, of the descendants of David; and the virgin's name was Mary. ²⁸And coming in, he said to her, "Greetings, favored one! The Lord *is* with you." ²⁹But she was very perplexed at

this statement, and kept pondering what kind of salutation this was. ³⁰The angel said to her, "Do not be afraid, Mary; for you have found favor with God. ³¹"And behold, you will conceive in your womb and bear a son, and you shall name Him Jesus. ³²"He will be great and will be called the Son of the Most High; and the Lord God will give Him the throne of His father David; ³³and He will reign over the house of Jacob forever, and His kingdom will have no end." ³⁴Mary said to the angel, "How can this be, since I am a virgin?" ³⁵The angel answered and said to her, "The Holy Spirit will come upon you, and the power of the Most High will overshadow you; and for that reason the holy Child shall be called the Son of God." (Luke 1:26-35)

• What was the name of Jesus' mother? Dig in verse 27.

• Mary was a virgin. She was not even married when the angel told her she would have a child. Verse 27 tell us she was going to marry a man by what name?

• What question does Mary ask the angel in verse 34?

You see from this verse that Mary could not understand how she was going to have a baby when she wasn't married yet.

• How does the angel answer her in verse 35?

Yes. The angel tells her that she is going to have God's Son! So this baby would have a human mother, Mary, AND a heavenly father, God, would be the father of this baby! This baby would be the Son of God!

2. Now let's look at what the Bible tells us about how Joseph found out what he was to do since the woman he wanted to marry was going to have God's Son!

¹⁸Now the birth of Jesus Christ was as follows: when His mother Mary had been betrothed to Joseph, before they came together she was found to be with child by the Holy Spirit. ¹⁹And Joseph her husband, being a righteous man and not wanting to disgrace her, planned to send her away secretly. ²⁰But when he had considered this, behold, an angel of the Lord appeared to him in a dream, saying, "Joseph, son of David, do not be afraid to take Mary as your wife; for the Child who has been conceived in her is of the Holy Spirit. ²¹"She will bear a Son; and you shall call His name Jesus, for He will save His people from their sins."(Matthew 1:18-21)

Who Is This Jesus?

Verse 18 tells us that Mary was betrothed to Joseph. Do you know what this means? Well, it is like being engaged. They were planning on being married.

In verses 18-19 we see that Joseph realized that Mary was going to have a baby and that he knew he was not the father. So he tried to decide what to do. These verses tell us he thought about putting her away secretly. This means that he thought maybe it would be best not to marry her and not to make a big public announcement about why he wouldn't.

BUT, what does the angel say to Joseph while he is trying to decide what to do? Look at verses 20-21 again. Write below what you think the angel means by what he says to Joseph.

• What does the angel tell Joseph to call the baby?

So we see that Joseph was to marry Mary and be like a father to Jesus. Do you know what a stepfather is? It is a man who marries a woman who already has a child, and he becomes like a father to the child because he cares for it and plays the role of father. This is the same situation Joseph found himself in with Jesus and Mary.

• What does the angel tell Joseph that Jesus will do? Look at verse 21 and write what you find below.

SPECIAL FIND!

The name "Son of Man" tells us Jesus was a real human being (Mark 8:31). God calling Jesus "son" (Mark 9:7) tells us that Jesus is truly God.

Well, you have had another long day of digging! I hope you are excited about all that you are learning because I surely am.

Of course, being older and wiser, I understand how important the treasures you are discovering will be to you for the rest of your life! So I am very glad that you are working so hard to understand. I know you will be glad too one day when all that you are uncovering begins to fit together in your mind and you see how it all makes so much sense!

But for today, know you have done a good job and that I am very, very proud of you!

Have a good rest of the day— and do something extra fun!

Truth Trackers: Jesus Our Savior and Friend

LAYER THREE: It Started in the Garden

Hello! I am excited about our digging today. We are getting close to the treasure we are after, so let's go!

1. We will begin our digging today where we left off yesterday. Do you remember the verses you read when the angel told Joseph about Jesus and what Jesus would do? Look back to the end of the last dig and read Matthew 1:18-21 again. Pay careful attention to verse 21.

2. Write below what the angel said about what Jesus would do.

3. Do you know what saving His people from their sins really means? If you go to church, you have heard teachers say that we—people—are sinners. But have you ever thought about what that means? And why do you need to be saved from sin? Let's see what we can uncover! I think it will take us digging through today and the next two layers to uncover all of the treasures we are looking for, so be patient and prepare to work hard. To find our answer, we have to go way back to the very beginning.

Read the verses from Genesis below.

¹⁶The LORD God commanded the man, saying, "From any tree of the garden you may eat freely; ¹⁷but from the tree of the knowledge of good and evil you shall not eat, for in the day that you eat from it you will surely die." ¹⁸Then the LORD God said, "It is not good for the man to be alone; I will make him a helper suitable for him." ¹⁹Out of the ground the LORD God formed every beast of the field and every bird of the sky, and brought *them* to the man to see what he would call them; and whatever the man called a living creature, that was its name. ²⁰The man gave names to all the cattle, and to the birds of the sky, and to every beast of the field, but for Adam there was not found a helper suitable for him. ²¹So the LORD God caused a deep sleep to fall upon the man, and he slept; then He took one of his ribs and closed up the flesh at that place. ²²The LORD God fashioned into a woman the rib which He had taken from the man, and brought her to the man. ²³The man said,

"This is now bone of my bones,
And flesh of my flesh;
She shall be called Woman,
Because she was taken out of Man."

²⁴For this reason a man shall leave his father and his mother, and be joined to his wife; and they shall become one flesh. ²⁵And the man and his wife were both naked and were not ashamed. (Genesis 2:16-25)

4. Who are three major characters you read about in these verses?

5. What does God tell the man in verse 17 about eating the fruit of the tree of the knowledge of good and evil?

6. What will happen if the fruit is eaten?

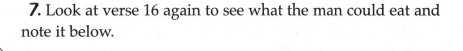

7. Look at verse 16 again to see what the man could eat and note it below.

Are you surprised to see he could eat from all of the trees except one?

8. After God made woman and gave her to the man, what does verse 25 tell you about them?

So today you have discovered that man and woman were created by God and given instructions about what they could and couldn't eat. And you saw too that they were naked and not ashamed.

Tomorrow our dig will introduce another major player in our story, and you will see how man became a sinner and why Jesus needed to come to earth.

Remember that we are trying to understand why Jesus needed to come to earth. That's why we're going back to the beginning.

You are learning amazing truths and are collecting very valuable treasures! Thank God now that He is helping you unearth truth that you can treasure all of your life!

Take a break. You deserve one! As for me, well...

LAYER FOUR: The BIG Problem!

Today we will continue to dig out treasures that will help you understand sin and why Jesus came to earth. Ready? Great, let's go because what we are going to dig out is so good we don't want to waste any time getting to it.

1. To see who our next major character is and what he does, read the following section of Scripture.

Truth Trackers: Jesus Our Savior and Friend

¹Now the serpent was more crafty than any beast of the field which the LORD God had made. And he said to the woman, "Indeed, has God said, 'You shall not eat from any tree of the garden'?" ²The woman said to the serpent, "From the fruit of the trees of the garden we may eat; ³but from the fruit of the tree which is in the middle of the garden, God has said, 'You shall not eat from it or touch it, or you will die.'" ⁴The serpent said to the woman, "You surely will not die! ⁵"For God knows that in the day you eat from it your eyes will be opened, and you will be like God, knowing good and evil." ⁶When the woman saw that the tree was good for food, and that it was a delight to the eyes, and that the tree was desirable to make *one* wise, she took from its fruit and ate; and she gave also to her husband with her, and he ate. ⁷Then the eyes of both of them were opened, and they knew that they were naked; and they sewed fig leaves together and made themselves loin coverings. ⁸They heard the sound of the LORD God walking in the garden in the cool of the day, and the man and his wife hid themselves from the presence of the LORD God among the trees of the garden. ⁹Then the LORD God called to the man, and said to him, "Where are you?" ¹⁰He said, "I heard the sound of You in the garden, and I was afraid because I was naked; so I hid myself." ¹¹And He said, "Who told you that you were naked? Have you eaten from the tree of which I commanded you not to eat?" ¹²The man said, "The woman whom You gave *to be* with me, she gave me from the tree, and I ate." ¹³Then the LORD God said to the woman, "What is this you have done?" And the woman said, "The serpent deceived me, and I ate." (Genesis 3:1-13)

2. Who comes on the scene in these verses?

3. Who is the serpent? Look at the verse below to find out his name. Circle his name when you see it.

⁹And the great dragon was thrown down, the serpent of old who is called the devil and Satan, who deceives the whole world; he was thrown down to the earth, and his angels were thrown down with him. (Revelation 12:9)

4. God told Adam and Eve not to eat the fruit or touch the tree that was in the middle of the garden because they would die if they did. What does the serpent say to Eve about this? (Look at verse 4.)

5. Does the woman eat the fruit? Does the man?

Who Is This Jesus?

6. Look in verse 7 to see what happened after they ate the fruit. Write it below.

7. Do you remember at the end of Layer Three reading Genesis 2:25 and noting how Adam and Eve felt about being naked? If you don't remember, look back. Note again how they felt at that point.

8. Now, we see that before they disobeyed what God had said and ate the fruit they were not ashamed. After they ate the fruit, they were ashamed to be naked. Read verse 10 again to see how Adam said he felt. What does he say?

9. Why were Adam and Eve ashamed and afraid?

Sin—doing what we know is wrong—will make us ashamed and afraid because we know we should not disobey!

10. How does God respond? Read verse 11. You will see that God asks a question that He already knows the answer to. He knows why they are afraid and ashamed, but He wants them to say the truth about what they did. Write what God says below.

11. Read verses 12-13 to see what Adam and Eve say to God. You will notice that they each blame someone for what they did. Write below who each blames.

Adam blames _____   Eve blames the _____

Can you understand how they felt? Isn't it always tempting to blame your brother or sister for the cookie that is missing instead of telling the truth if you took it?

12. One last question before we clean up for the day. Do you remember in Layer Three when you read Genesis 2:17 and saw what God said would happen if they ate the fruit? Look back again at the verse on page 26. What did God say would happen? Write it below and we'll talk about it tomorrow.

I know you must be tired! It has been a tough layer to dig through,
but you made it! You now see how sin began. It all started with a man
and a woman who did not do what God said to do—who disobeyed.

And you saw, too, that Adam and Eve had plenty of trees to eat from.
They did not need the fruit. They simply wanted what God told them they
could not have. Then you saw how they were ashamed and afraid.

Tomorrow, we will see what God says to each of the players in the story,
and we will see what the Bible says about why Jesus came to earth.

LAYER FIVE: The Gift Jesus Brings

Well, we are on the last layer of Dig Two today. It is hard to believe. It has gone by so quickly. We will have to dig hard again today, but when we finish you will be very happy with all you have uncovered this week, and I believe you will understand not only who Jesus really is but also why He came to earth.

1. Let's look today at a different part of the Bible to try and understand what happened as a result of the sin in the garden. Sin separated man from God. The Bible says in Romans 5:19, that "…through the one man's disobedience, the many were made sinners,…"

2. Look again at the verse above. Who do you think the "one man" who disobeyed is?

3. What does Romans 5:19 say happened because of Adam's disobedience?

4. Yes, you are right. When Adam disobeyed God, it affected all mankind. Read the beginning of Romans 6:23 to see what the Bible says is the penalty or wage for sin. Circle the penalty for sin in the verse below.

²³For the wages of sin is death…

5. There it is! Sin brings death. Think back now to the end of Layer Four where I asked you to look at Genesis 2:17 again to see what God said would happen if they ate the fruit. Do you remember what God said? If not, look back to the last question of Layer Four. What did you find?

Who Is This Jesus?

Yes, death was a result of sin. But, you may say, "They did not die!" They were ashamed and afraid, but they were still alive. But now think with me for a moment.

Their bodies may still have been alive, but can you remember where they were after they ate the fruit when God came into the garden? Yes, they were hiding.

They were hiding because something had separated them from God. They were now afraid of the One Who made them, Who gave them life. Sin caused them to fear God. So they may not have died physically, but they did die in their spirit or spiritually. Just like God said they would! This spiritual death separated them from God.

6. Adam and Eve are not the only ones who died spiritually because of their sin. Read 1 Corinthians 15:21-22 below and circle the word that tells you how many died because of Adam's sin.

²¹For since by a man *came* death, by a man also *came* the resurrection of the dead. ²²For as in Adam all die, so also in Christ all will be made alive.

7. Now you may think this all sounds like really bad news, so let's look now at the good news! Read 1 Corinthians 15:22 above again. Read carefully again and see what the verse says about those who are in Christ. Note what you learn.

8. Now take the time to look up Romans 6:23 in your Bible and write out the entire verse below. You looked at part of that verse in number 3 above, but now I want you to read and write the entire verse.

9. Look back at the verse you wrote out in number 8 and circle what the Bible tells you is God's free gift to those who are in Christ Jesus.

10. In number 1, you looked at part of Romans 5:19 to see what happened to man because of Adam's disobedience. But now let's look at the rest of the verse to see what happened because of Christ's obedience—"even so through the obedience of the One the many will be made righteous." Underline what can happen because of Jesus—called the One in this verse.

Now, that is good news, isn't it? Because of Jesus, you can be righteous, you can become a believer and not die—spiritually. And even though you will die physically one day, you will live forever in heaven with God, Jesus, and the Holy Spirit!

Truth Trackers: Jesus Our Savior and Friend

So can you see why Jesus came to earth? He came so sinners would not have to die. In a dig that is coming up, we will uncover more treasures that will explain to you more about how Jesus made a way for you to be a saint and not a sinner. But today you just need to understand that Jesus came to save you from sin and death!

11. Look on page 33 to see the last fun part of our dig! Digging for Dots will reveal one last treasure—it's a great one!

You've reached the bottom of Dig Two! You have worked hard, and even though you may not know it now, you have a pile of treasures that will be valuable to you all of your life. And one day, you will be very glad that you worked diligently now to uncover these treasures.

I will look forward to seeing you soon in Dig Three.
But don't forget the two sections below! I'm off...

Truth Treasures for the Week

1.

2.

3.

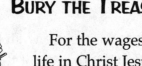

Bury the Treasure:

For the wages of sin is death, but the gift of God is eternal life in Christ Jesus our Lord (Roman 6:23).

Who Is This Jesus?

Before and After Jesus Saves You

Two words are buried in this letter puzzle. The first word describes who you are before Jesus saves you. In seven moves, can you go to the letters that spell out what that word is?

After Jesus saves you, you become a new person in Christ. In six moves, find the letters that spell out your new name when you believe in Jesus and He saves you.

Once you find the words, write each word on the line provided. (For a hint about the two words you're looking for, go back and read number 10 in Layer Five.)

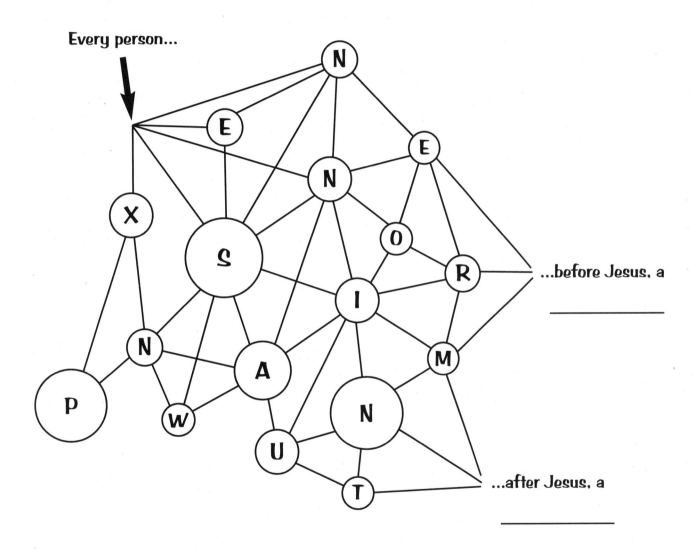

solution on page 194

33

Dig 3

The Start of Something Big!

Tools of the Trade

1. Colored pencils
2. Pen or pencil
3. Encounters with Jesus on pages 18-19
4. The Timeline of the Life of Christ on pages 191-192
5. A Puzzle of People and Places on page 52

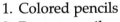

Directions for Diggers

In Dig Two, we took a break from looking at the life of Jesus to see exactly who He was, and is, and why He came to earth. And in this dig, we will start again to look at Jesus' life by picking up where we left off in Dig One.

You will remember that Dig One was a quick look at the birth of Jesus, and now we want to learn what the Bible says about His life as a boy and see what we can discover about the work He did as a man. You know—a look from ground level instead of our view from the Eiffel Tower! We will see how He prepares to accomplish some of the special things He came to earth to do. And we will talk about the men Jesus asked to help Him in these tasks.

It will be an exciting dig since it will uncover neat truths about the God-Man called Jesus.

Truth Trackers: Jesus Our Savior and Friend

LAYER ONE: Angels and Shepherds Hear the News

In Dig One you read the sections of the Bible that talked about how Mary and Joseph found out that Jesus was going to be born. You also read about how Jesus was born and how the king who was ruling at His birth wanted to kill Him.

Today before we go on to see more about Jesus as a boy and a man, let's take a little time to dig more into the chapters of the Bible that talk about His birth. We won't spend much time digging here, but I think you will find some treasures that are important to see.

1. Go to the Treasure Map on pages 187-190 and read Luke 2:1-16 which begins on page 189. Answer the questions that follow.

• Read verses 4-6 again. What is the name of the town where Jesus was born?

• You read about Mary and Joseph having to go to this little town to register for the census. Do you know what a census is? (Look at the Special Find box below to remind yourself.) There was a census in the year 2000 in the United States.

The census we read about in the Bible required that the people go to certain towns to give the information for the census. Joseph had to go to Bethlehem.

And while Mary and Joseph were in Bethlehem, what happens? Look in verses 6-7.

SPECIAL FIND!

A census is a count of people living in a certain area. The government takes the count so it knows how many people are in the area. The government wants to know so they can plan better ways to take care of the people. The count of people helps with planning for enough schools and teachers, for large enough parks for everyone to enjoy, and for improving roads for everyone to drive on.

• Verse 7 tells you where Mary and Joseph were staying when the baby was born. Why were they there?

• In verses 8-9, who did the angels appear to and tell about the birth of this baby?

• What area of the country were these men in when the angels appeared to them? You may have to read carefully to understand what the verse says, but I know you can get it! I'll help you out by telling you to look in verse 8.

• What were these men doing when the angels appeared to them?

The Start of Something Big!

• What do these men do after they hear the news of this birth?

2. Look again at your Treasure Map on pages 187-190 in the back of the book and read the section of Scripture from Matthew 2:1-12 and answer the following questions.

• Who was the king when Jesus was born?

• How did the king feel about the birth of Jesus? Look in verse 3.

• Look at verse 8 to see what King Herod told the magi, or "wise men," to do. Write what he said below.

SPECIAL FIND!

The stable was a place where animals were kept and fed. The stables in Bethlehem were usually caves cut out of the rock. The stable where Jesus was born was probably one of these caves.

And the manger where they laid Jesus after He was born was really a stone box! The box was used to hold food for the animals.

• After the wise men found Jesus and visited with Mary and Joseph, do they go back to King Herod like he had asked them to do? Why? Look in verse 12 if you need help remembering.

• Now read Matthew 2:16 below and see what King Herod did. Write what you learn.

16Then when Herod saw that he had been tricked by the magi, he became very enraged, and sent and slew [killed] all the male children who were in Bethlehem and all its vicinity, from two years old and under, according to the time which he had determined from the magi.

3. Now let's read one last section from the Bible for today. Hang in there, because you are almost finished digging for the day!
Read Matthew 2:13-15, 19-23 below and then answer the questions that follow.

13Now when they had gone, behold, an angel of the Lord appeared to Joseph in a dream and said, "Get up! Take the Child and His mother and flee to Egypt, and remain there until I tell you; for Herod is going to search for the Child to destroy Him." **14**So Joseph got up and took the Child and His mother while it was still night, and left for Egypt. **15**He remained there until the death of Herod. *This was* to fulfill what had been spoken by the Lord through the prophet: "OUT OF EGYPT I CALLED MY SON."

19But when Herod died, behold, an angel of the Lord appeared in a dream to Joseph in Egypt, and said, **20**"Get up, take the Child and His mother, and go into the land of Israel; for those who sought the Child's life are dead." **21**So Joseph got up, took the Child and His mother, and came into the land of Israel. **22**But when he heard that Archelaus was reigning over Judea in place of his father Herod, he was afraid to go there. Then after being warned *by God* in a dream, he left for the regions of Galilee, **23**and came and lived in a city called Nazareth. *This was* to fulfill what was spoken through the prophets: "He shall be called a Nazarene."

• In verse 13, where does the angel tell Joseph to go?

• Why does the angel tell Joseph to make this journey?

• What event is recorded in verse 19 that makes it okay for Mary, Joseph, and Jesus to leave Egypt?

• How do they know it is okay to leave now? Who appears to tell them to go?

• Where do they go? Verse 21 tells you.

4. Look at the map and think about where Jesus was born, where the angel told Joseph to take his family, and where they moved after Herod died. Now, use one of your colored pencils to mark where Jesus was born.

Next mark Egypt where they fled with Him.

Last, mark the city they go to after Herod dies.

Now look at your marks and you can see Jesus' travels as a baby boy.

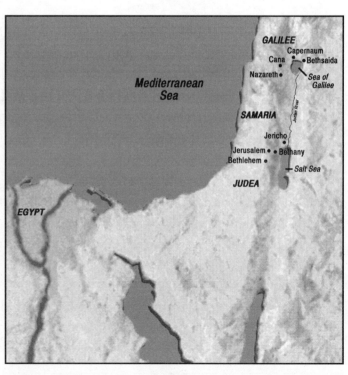

5. Also look on the Encounters with Jesus drawing on pages 18-19 and circle the city where Jesus lived with His parents and grew up. Color this part of the drawing.

Isn't it fun to remember some of the details of Jesus' birth and to look at them a little closer? Just think how much more you will understand about the "Christmas Story" this year—because you have taken time to see the details for yourself!

I hope that you thought about how God spoke to the shepherds, to Joseph, to the Wise Men as you read today. We are going to talk later in a dig about how God talks to us—and about how we should talk to Him. But when we get there, I will want you to remember how He spoke to these people.

And will you think of just one more neat thing with me for a second? What were the shepherds doing when the angel appeared to them? Yes, they were tending—watching—their sheep. What do shepherds usually do? Right again! They tend sheep.

Did you think about the fact that these men were doing what they did every day when the angel appeared to them? They were not sitting under a tree looking into the heavens and hoping God would talk to them! They were doing what they did every day. They were doing what they were supposed to do. And God came to them and talked with them through an angel.

Pretty neat to think about the fact that you can do what you are supposed to do and God can find a way to talk to you, isn't it? Lots to think about!

> **SPECIAL FIND!**
>
> You may not remember where Mary was living when she found out she was going to have a baby. Look back in Dig One and read Luke 1:26 (on page 10) to find out. You also see a hint about where Mary and Joseph were from in Luke 2:39. You may want to see if you can find this clue.

You are awesome! Have a fun treat to celebrate your hard work. And, I'll see you in Layer Two.

LAYER TWO: Jesus Is Missing!

As you know, there is much in the Bible about Jesus' birth. And we have had a fun time looking at some of what is recorded about His birth. But what you are going to discover today is that there is not much in the Bible about Him as a boy or young man.

But because we want to understand all we can about Jesus' life, we will look at what the Bible says about this time and see what we can learn. Ready? Great! Let's go.

1. Read Luke 2:40-52 below and then answer the questions that follow.

40The Child continued to grow and become strong, increasing in wisdom; and the grace of God was upon Him.
41Now His parents went to Jerusalem every year at the Feast of the Passover. **42**And when He became twelve, they went up *there* according to the custom of the Feast; **43**and

as they were returning, after spending the full number of days, the boy Jesus stayed behind in Jerusalem. But His parents were unaware of it, **44**but supposed Him to be in the caravan, and went a day's journey; and they *began* looking for Him among their relatives and acquaintances. **45**When they did not find Him, they returned to Jerusalem looking for Him. **46**Then, after three days they found Him in the temple, sitting in the midst of the teachers, both listening to them and asking them questions. **47**And all who heard Him were amazed at His understanding and His answers. **48**When they saw Him, they were astonished; and His mother said to Him, "Son, why have You treated us this way? Behold, Your father and I have been anxiously looking for You." **49**And He said to them, "Why is it that you were looking for Me? Did you not know that I had to be in My Father's *house?*" **50**But they did not understand the statement which He had made to them. **51**And He went down with them and came to Nazareth, and He continued in subjection to them; and His mother treasured all *these* things in her heart. **52**And Jesus kept increasing in wisdom and stature, and in favor with God and men.

- What does verse 40 tell you about Jesus? I'll help you below.

    He continued to _____.

    He became _____.

    He increased in _____.

    The _____ _____ _____ was upon Him.

So we can learn that Jesus grew up just like you are growing up and that He was becoming strong as He grew to be a man.

SPECIAL FIND!

The Temple was built in Jerusalem on Mount Moriah. King Solomon built the First Temple so that God would have a dwelling place on earth. It was a very large and extremely beautiful building where the Jewish people went to worship their God.

We can also see two things that may seem a bit unusual for a boy. One is that He was filled with wisdom. Usually we think of people being wise when they are older and have lived a long time and learned a lot about life. But we see here that Jesus was already filled with wisdom.

The second unusual thing we learn is that the grace of God was on Him. This means that there was something inside Him—in His heart—that made Him act differently from other boys.

- Look again in verse 42 and write below how old Jesus was when He went to the Temple with His parents.

- At the age of 12 Jewish boys were considered old enough to keep God's Law. The Old Testament said that

The Start of Something Big!

Jewish men were supposed to go to the Temple to worship on Passover, one of the holy days the Jewish people celebrate. Now that Jesus was 12, He went to Jerusalem for this Passover. This was a normal part of growing up, so there was nothing surprising about the fact that Jesus was in the Temple.

But when He did not leave with His parents and they had to go back for Him, the answer He gives them about why He stayed behind is surprising! What did He say to His mother in verse 49? Write your answer below.

• Did they understand what He meant by His response?

It may be hard even for you to really understand what Jesus meant, but I think what we can learn is that even as a boy of 12 Jesus knew who He was. He knew Mary and Joseph were His earthly parents, but He was aware that God was His heavenly Father. And that is why He called the Temple His Father's house.

• Read verse 51 carefully and slowly and see what you learn about how Jesus acted toward His earthly parents. Write the verse out below.

What does "subjection" mean? Do you know? Well, believe it or not, it means to be obedient!

Don't you think that it is amazing that Jesus knew His father was God and that He still knew He should be obedient to Joseph and Mary? God *was* His father. God of all the Universe! God who was all-powerful! God who is omnipresent—everywhere at once! God who knows everything, every thought of every person! God was Jesus' father, but Jesus still obeyed the mother and father God had given Him on earth.

What about you? Don't you think you should look at Jesus' example and be obedient to your parents? You may think sometimes that you know better than your parents about what you should be able to do or have, but the next time you have a thought like that, think of this: God gave you your parents, and He wants you to obey them!

2. Now take a moment to look at Encounters with Jesus on pages 18-19. Do you remember from what you read where the Temple was? Yes, Jerusalem. Circle this city, and color this part of the drawing.

3. Also turn to the Timeline of the Life of Christ on pages 191-192 and mark the event you uncovered in this layer.

Well, that seems like enough to think about for one day, doesn't it? Maybe tonight you can take a few minutes and share with your parents what you dug up today. Tell them that you want to be obedient and that you will ask God to help you understand how you can be more obedient.

Now, ask God to show you. And remember that you should be willing to do what He shows you.

Okay, see you tomorrow! I am off for a swim. Hope you're going to have some fun too!

LAYER THREE: Jesus Starts His Ministry

Today we get to start digging out treasure about Jesus as a young man. We will uncover some of the things He begins to do. These are things that God, His heavenly Father, sent Him to earth to do. When people talk about this part of Jesus' life, they use the term "ministry." They say that Jesus began His ministry. All they really mean is that He started to do the things that God asked Him to do while He was on the earth.

Remember that Jesus came to earth so that mankind would have a way out of their sin. But Jesus had to live in a way that would help people realize who He was and why He came, and that is what we will get to look at now—how He lived!

1. Let's begin today by reading Luke 3:21-23a.

²¹Now when all the people were baptized, Jesus was also baptized, and while He was praying, heaven was opened, ²²and the Holy Spirit descended upon Him in bodily form like a dove, and a voice came out of heaven, "You are My beloved Son, in You I am well-pleased." ²³When He began His ministry, Jesus Himself was about thirty years of age…

- How old was Jesus when He began His ministry?

- What is Jesus doing in the verses you just read?

Have you ever seen anyone get baptized? People are baptized when they want to show others that they believe Jesus is the Son of God and that they want to live like He lived.

Jesus was baptized so that people would know who He was. Remember that He had to show people who He was and why He came so that they could believe. Let's look at what John the Baptist says so we can understand more about why Jesus did this.

John was Jesus' cousin, and God had asked John to do some special things too. One of the things God had asked John to do was to watch for Jesus and to point others to Jesus when John saw Him. Let's read John 1:29-34.

The Start of Something Big!

²⁹The next day he saw Jesus coming to him and said, "Behold, the Lamb of God who takes away the sin of the world! ³⁰"This is He on behalf of whom I said, 'After me comes a Man who has a higher rank than I, for He existed before me.' ³¹"I did not recognize Him, but so that He might be manifested to Israel, I came baptizing in water." ³²John testified saying, "I have seen the Spirit descending as a dove out of heaven, and He remained upon Him. ³³"I did not recognize Him, but He who sent me to baptize in water said to me, 'He upon whom you see the Spirit descending and remaining upon Him, this is the One who baptizes in the Holy Spirit.' ³⁴"I myself have seen, and have testified that this is the Son of God."

• Read verse 31 and write below why John said he was baptizing people.

So you can see that John was baptizing so that Jesus would be revealed to Israel—so that the people would know He was different from other men.

• Look back at verse 32 and write below what came out of heaven when John baptized Jesus.

• Now look again at what John said in verse 34. Who did John say Jesus was?

• Why did John think Jesus was the Son of God? Think very hard.

Yes, because in verse 33 John tells us that God had told him how he would know that Jesus was Jesus. He had been told the Spirit would come down on Jesus when He was baptized. John tells us in verse 32 that the Spirit did come down as a dove when he baptized Jesus!

2. Just after Jesus is baptized, He goes away for 40 days to pray. He is preparing Himself for what is coming ahead. Read Luke 4:1-13 below and answer the questions that follow. This digging will take some extra energy on your part, but I know you can do it. And I know what you will uncover is really worth the effort.

¹Jesus, full of the Holy Spirit, returned from the Jordan and was led around by the Spirit in the wilderness ²for forty days, being tempted by the devil. And He ate nothing during those days, and when they had ended, He became hungry. ³And the devil said to Him, "If You are the Son of God, tell this stone to become bread." ⁴And Jesus answered him, "It is written, 'MAN SHALL NOT LIVE ON BREAD ALONE.'"

⁵And he led Him up and showed Him all the kingdoms of the world in a moment of time. ⁶And the devil said to Him, "I will give You all this domain and its glory; for it has been handed over to me, and I give it to whomever I wish. ⁷"Therefore if You worship before me, it shall all be Yours." ⁸Jesus answered him, "It is written, 'YOU SHALL WORSHIP THE LORD YOUR GOD AND SERVE HIM ONLY.'" ⁹And he led Him to Jerusalem and had Him stand on the pinnacle of the temple, and said to Him, "If You are the Son of God, throw Yourself down from here; ¹⁰for it is written, 'HE WILL COMMAND HIS ANGELS CONCERNING YOU TO GUARD YOU,' ¹¹and, 'ON *their* HANDS THEY WILL BEAR YOU UP, SO THAT YOU WILL NOT STRIKE YOUR FOOT AGAINST A STONE.'" ¹²And Jesus answered and said to him, "It is said, 'YOU SHALL NOT PUT THE LORD YOUR GOD TO THE TEST.'" ¹³When the devil had finished every temptation, he left Him until an opportune time.

- Who tempted Jesus in the wilderness? Look at verse 2.

- Do you remember who tempted Eve in the garden?

Can you see that the devil likes to try and ruin what God wants to do?

- Look at verse 3 and write out the first thing that the devil tries to get Jesus to do.

- Was Jesus the Son of God? Could He have turned the stone to bread? Remember, He was hungry. The Bible tells us He had not been eating.

- What is the next temptation the devil brings to Jesus in verses 5-7?

Did you realize that when Adam and Eve sinned, Satan won the rule of this earth? Because Adam and Eve disobeyed God, God would not let man rule the earth any longer. So Satan is telling the truth when he says the kingdoms are his.

But what Jesus knows is that one day soon that will end. Jesus knows that God has a plan, and He is willing to wait and let God do things His way and in His timing. Being willing to wait on God gave Jesus the power He needed to resist the temptations of the devil.

- What is the last temptation you see in verses 9-11?

The Start of Something Big!

The pinnacle of the Temple is the top corner formed where the southern and eastern walls meet. If someone jumped from that point, they would be jumping down about 700 feet. And they would be jumping onto solid rock!

Again Satan teases Jesus about being the Son of God and tries to get Him to do something foolish to prove it. But Jesus knows the truth and does not have to prove who He is to Satan in this way!

Now, because we are running out of time and I know you are tired, let me just tell you that every time Jesus answers Satan, He quotes from the Bible. If you want to see these responses for yourself, I'll put them in a chart for you.

TEMPTATION	JESUS' RESPONSE	WHERE IN BIBLE
Stone to bread	Man does not live by bread alone v4	Deuteronomy 8:3
Domain if worship	You shall worship the Lord your God…v8	Deuteronomy 6:13
If Son of God, throw yourself down	You shall not put…God to the test v12	Deuteronomy 6:16

It is an important lesson for us! We need to know the Word of God. Every time Jesus answered Satan with God's Word, Satan dropped the temptation and tried another one. But with each temptation, Jesus knew the truth of God's Word, and Satan knew he had to give up!

This is why I am so excited that you are taking the time to unearth truth from the Word of God! You need to know truth to stand against the lies that will be thrown at you from lots of directions! And you are well on you way to learning the truths of the Word! See why I am so proud of you?

3. You should be able to locate the river where Jesus was baptized on the Encounters with Jesus drawing on pages 18-19. Circle it, and color this part of the drawing.

4. And last, go to the Timeline of the Life of Christ on pages 191-192 and note the two events you unearthed today.

I wish we could keep going a little deeper, but I know you have to be tired of digging. We have uncovered sooo much today. Let's stop and we will keep on learning about Jesus' ministry tomorrow!

Thank you for hanging in there with me today. Put your tools up and take a well-deserved break! You are a trooper!

Truth Trackers: Jesus Our Savior and Friend

LAYER FOUR: His Hometown Didn't Understand

Today, our digging will go quickly. I bet you are glad after such a big dig yesterday! Let's get started, and we will uncover the rest of the story of how Jesus prepared to begin His ministry.

You may think the last phase of Jesus' preparation is a little strange because He goes to His hometown to try and help the people He grew up with understand who He really is. But we will see why He does this later.

1. Read Luke 4:14-20, 28-30 and then answer the questions that follow.

14And Jesus returned to Galilee in the power of the Spirit, and news about Him spread through all the surrounding district. **15**And He *began* teaching in their synagogues and was praised by all. **16**And He came to Nazareth, where He had been brought up; and as was His custom, He entered the synagogue on the Sabbath, and stood up to read. **17**And the book of the prophet Isaiah was handed to Him. And He opened the book and found the place where it was written, **18** "THE SPIRIT OF THE LORD IS UPON ME, BECAUSE HE ANOINTED ME TO PREACH THE GOSPEL TO THE POOR. HE HAS SENT ME TO PROCLAIM RELEASE TO THE CAPTIVES, AND RECOVERY OF SIGHT TO THE BLIND, TO SET FREE THOSE WHO ARE OPPRESSED, **19** TO PROCLAIM THE FAVORABLE YEAR OF THE LORD." **20**And He closed the book, gave it back to the attendant and sat down; and the eyes of all in the synagogue were fixed on Him…

28And all *the people* in the synagogue were filled with rage as they heard these things; **29**and they got up and drove Him out of the city, and led Him to the brow of the hill on which their city had been built, in order to throw Him down the cliff. **30**But passing through their midst, He went His way.

• What Old Testament book does He read from in the synagogue? Verse 17 tells you.

Yes, He reads a part of the Scripture from the book of Isaiah. And the people get very upset with Him because they understand that what He read meant that He was claiming to be God! They knew that He was telling them that He thought He was the Messiah whom they had been waiting for to come to earth!

They were angry because this synagogue was in His hometown and these people knew Him as Mary and Joseph's son. They could not believe that He would claim to be God. They felt it was wrong and foolish!

The Start of Something Big!

• Some people were extremely upset. Look again in verse 29 to see what they tried to do to Him. Write what you find.

• Did their attempt to get rid of Jesus work? Write out verse 30.

Jesus understood why they were upset. He knew they were confused by what He had said. But He had come home to try and help them understand. He loved these people in a special way because He had grown up with them.

But He knew who He was. And He knew He had a job to do. So He leaves His hometown to go to another part of the country to begin the work God asked Him to do.

Tomorrow we will see how He began that work.

SPECIAL FIND!

The Jewish people had been promised a Messiah in the Old Testament. But they had decided that this man would be a military conqueror. They certainly did not think Jesus was this Messiah.

What they did not understand was that the word *Messiah* really meant "God with us."

Now you know that is exactly what Jesus was. He was God come to earth as a man. He was the God Man!

LAYER FIVE: Twelve Trusted Men

Part of what Jesus did in order to begin His work was to choose 12 men to be His special friends while He was on earth. They were men who spent lots of time with Him. He taught these men spiritual truths and showed them how to help other people.

Jesus wanted these men to know and understand about helping people because He knew the people they helped would want to know why these men had helped them. And He knew that their curiosity would open a way for them to tell other people about Him and who He was and why He had come to earth.

1. Let's see who these men were. Read Mark 3:13-19.

¹³And He went up on the mountain and summoned those whom He Himself wanted, and they came to Him. ¹⁴And He appointed twelve, so that they would be with Him and that He *could* send them out to preach, ¹⁵and to have authority to cast out the demons. ¹⁶And He appointed the twelve: Simon (to whom He gave the name Peter), ¹⁷and James, the *son* of Zebedee, and John the brother of James (to them He gave the name Boanerges, which means, "Sons of Thunder"); ¹⁸and Andrew, and Philip, and Bartholomew, and Matthew, and Thomas, and James the son of Alphaeus, and Thaddaeus, and Simon the Zealot; ¹⁹and Judas Iscariot, who betrayed Him.

- Make a list of the 12 men:

  1   7

  2   8

  3   9

  4   10

  5   11

  6   12

- Read verses 14 and 15 again and list the three things you see about why Jesus appointed these men. I'll help you a bit.

  That they would _____ _____ _____

  That He could send them out _____ _____

  And to have authority to cast out the _____

As you can see from this list, the things we talked about earlier were correct—He wanted to teach them how to help people!

- Read Mark 6: 7a, 12-13 below and see what Jesus has the 12 men doing.

7And He summoned the twelve and began to send them out in pairs, and gave them authority over the unclean spirits; **12**They went out and preached that *men* should repent. **13**And they were casting out many demons and were anointing with oil many sick people and healing them.

So note below what the men were doing. Look in verses 12-13. Again, I'll give you some help.

  They preached that men should _____

  They were _____ out many _____

  And were anointing with oil _____ _____ _____ and were _____ them.

48

The Start of Something Big!

2. Do you wonder who these men were before Jesus found them? We won't take long enough to discover something about each of them, but let's just look at what several of the men were doing before Jesus came along and asked them to follow Him.

• Let's see what you can find out about Matthew. Read Matthew 9:9-12 and note below what job Matthew had when Jesus asked him to come with Him.

9And as Jesus passed on from there, He saw a man, called Matthew, sitting in the tax office; and He said to him, "Follow Me!" And he rose, and followed Him. **10**And it happened that as he was reclining *at the table* in the house, behold many tax-gatherers and sinners came and were dining with Jesus and His disciples. **11**And when the Pharisees saw *this*, they said to His disciples, "Why is your Teacher eating with the tax-gatherers and sinners?" **12**But when He heard this, He said, "*It is* not those who are healthy who need a physician, but those who are sick."

SPECIAL FIND!

The Pharisees were religious men who studied the Bible and wanted to please God, but they did not really understand what they read in the Scriptures. These men tried to please God by being better than other people. When Jesus showed them that they were wrong, they hated Him and became His enemies.

• What did the Pharisees have to say about Jesus eating with the tax collectors?

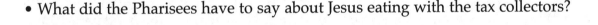

You get the idea, don't you, that the Pharisees did not think very highly of the tax collectors? You see that Jesus called Matthew even though Matthew had a job that the religious leaders did not respect.

• Read Matthew 4:18-20 and see what two others of the disciples were doing when Jesus asked them to come with Him. Write below what these two men did for a living.

18Now as Jesus was walking by the Sea of Galilee, He saw two brothers, Simon who was called Peter, and Andrew his brother, casting a net into the sea; for they were fishermen. **19**And He said to them, "Follow Me, and I will make you fishers of men." **20**Immediately they left their nets and followed Him.

SPECIAL FIND!

The word "disciple" means student or learner. Jesus trained these men to teach and preach the gospel—the story about Him and what He came to do. The disciples were ordinary men who were doing their jobs until Jesus asked them to come with Him and help do God's work.

Truth Trackers: Jesus Our Savior and Friend

• What did Jesus tell these two men that He would teach them to do?

• Read Mark 3:19 below. Look to see what you can find out about the disciple called Judas. What do you see that he is going to do?

¹⁹and Judas Iscariot, who betrayed Him.

Isn't it sad to think about the fact that one of the men Jesus asked to work with Him was going to betray Him in the end? Judas was going to lead the police to Jesus and have Him arrested so that He could be crucified.

You see that these men were normal men doing what they did every day when Jesus found them. You can see too how Jesus wanted these men to learn to help others and how He wanted them to understand all that was going to happen in the days to come. Do you have friends who are special to you the way these men were special to Jesus?

Do you want to be someone Jesus can trust to do His work? Do you want Jesus to show you how you can help others so that they will want to know why you are different? So they will want to know Who makes you different?

Think of a boy or girl you know who most other kids do not like or do not spend time with. Do you think Jesus would want you to be nice to that person? To spend some time with that guy or girl? Think about it and ask Him. He will tell you. And He will show you what to do if you are willing.

3. Go to the timeline on pages 191-192 and note the event you uncovered today.

4. Oh, yeah, if you want to have a little fun today before you close your book, you'll see a puzzle to dig through on page 52. See if you can get it quickly!

Well, you have reached the bottom of this dig. It has been some dig, hasn't it? Ask God to help you understand any treasure you uncovered that you still do not understand.

I think you are amazing, and I will be looking forward to seeing you in Dig Four!

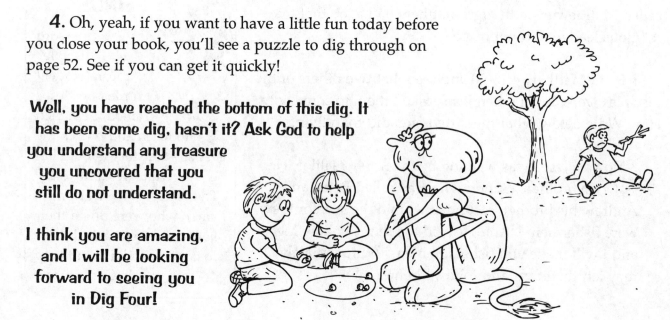

The Start of Something Big!

Truth Treasures for the Week

1.

2.

3.

Bury the Treasure:

Behold, I bring you good news of great joy which shall be for all the people; for today in the city of David there has been born for you a Savior, who is Christ the Lord (Luke 2:10-11).

Truth Trackers

A Puzzle of People and Places

You've been studying about many places and people in Jesus' early growing up years. Below are 14 people and places that Jesus knew. The words are all mixed up. Put two puzzle pieces together to form one word. Use one piece from each side to form your word. I've given you a sample to get you started. Good luck with this puzzle!

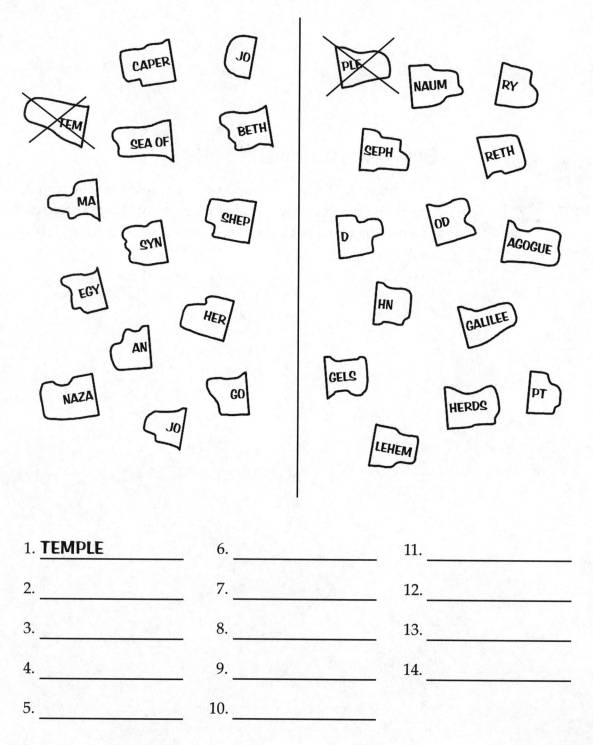

1. **TEMPLE**
2. _____
3. _____
4. _____
5. _____
6. _____
7. _____
8. _____
9. _____
10. _____
11. _____
12. _____
13. _____
14. _____

solution on page 194

Dig 4

How to Become a Follower

Tools of the Trade

1. Colored pencils
2. Pen or pencil
3. Dictionary
4. Encounters with Jesus on pages 18-19
5. Name That Disciple! game on page 67

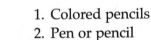

Directions for Diggers

You are doing well! You have completed three digs, and I know you must be excited about some of the treasure you have uncovered! It is so much fun to go on the digs with you that I have been ready since early this morning to get started. Hope you are as eager as I am to get going!

This week we will dig around and learn about some of the men and women that Jesus met and see how He talked with them. The treasures that you discover will help you understand more about other people—and it will help you be the kind of person that others will want to be around.

One of the main reasons I want you to come on this dig with me is to see that Jesus was willing to talk with *all* people, no matter who they were—no matter how rich or poor they were, no matter how sinful they were, no matter how confused or lost they were. Jesus loved *all* people!

Okay, check in with headquarters and let's go!

Truth Trackers: Jesus Our Savior and Friend

LAYER ONE: Seeking After Truth

Today, we want to meet a man who came to Jesus and asked a very important question. His name was Nicodemus, and he was a religious leader in Israel. He was a man that every one in Israel would expect to know all about religious things. Like you would expect your pastor or a Bible teacher to know about the things of God.

But Nicodemus realizes that Jesus is different from him and from the other religious men he knows, and so he goes to visit Jesus and asks Him some questions. I want you to read a section of Scripture with me, but I want you to do something a little differently as you read today.

I want you to do some art as you go. There are some key words you should mark. Key words are words that will help you see what is really being said and that will help you understand what you are reading is really about! I will list them for you and show you how I would mark them. You may have a different way you want to mark each word, and that is okay. You can just look at what I am doing to get an idea.

This is a good time to use your colored pencils. Even though you will draw a symbol, you can also use color. For instance, each time I see the word *Son*, I use a red pencil and draw the symbol of a cross over it, so that it looks like the one below.

You get the idea? Okay, here are my examples for you to use as a guideline or to give you ideas:

Why don't you take a moment and decide how you will mark each word and decide what color you will use. You see sometimes I use a circle or box. When I do I always use the same color, so I have a red circle over kingdom and a blue box around born or born again, and so on. Practice here on each word so you are sure of what you want to do:

God   Son   Kingdom   world   born / born again   spirit

Now that you know what words to mark and have decided how you will mark them, read the verses from the Gospel of John below and mark the words listed above as you read so that you can see what Jesus and Nicodemus talked about.

1Now there was a man of the Pharisees, named Nicodemus, a ruler of the Jews; **2**this man came to Jesus by night and said to Him, "Rabbi, we know that You have come from God *as* a teacher; for no one can do these signs that You do unless God is with him." ³Jesus answered and said to him, "Truly, truly, I say to you, unless one is born again he cannot see the kingdom of God." ⁴Nicodemus said to Him, "How can a man be born when he is old? He cannot enter a second time into his mother's womb and be born, can he?" ⁵Jesus answered, "Truly, truly, I say to you, unless one is born of water and the Spirit he cannot enter into the kingdom of God. ⁶"That which is born of the flesh is flesh, and that which is born of the Spirit is spirit. ⁷"Do not be amazed that I said to you, 'You must be born again.' ⁸"The wind blows where it wishes and you hear the sound of it, but do not know where it comes from and where it is going; so is everyone who is born of the Spirit." ⁹Nicodemus said to Him, "How can these things be?" ¹⁶"For God so loved the world, that He gave His only begotten Son, that whoever believes in Him shall not perish, but have eternal life. ¹⁷"For God did not send the Son into the world to judge the world, but that the world might be saved through Him."

1. Maybe you should read John 3:1-9, 16-17 again and be sure you marked all of the key words. Then, tomorrow, we will talk about what you saw.

You've read a long section of Scripture and worked hard to mark the key words. So since you've worked so hard digging out these words, take a break, and I'll see you next layer!

LAYER TWO: A Second Chance...A Second Birth

Yesterday you met a man named Nicodemus, who was a very important man in Israel. To try and understand more about his meeting with Jesus, today we will dig through some questions. If you need to look back at what you uncovered yesterday to help you in today's dig, that'll be fine. Let's go!

1. Look back in verse two and write down below *when* Nicodemus came to Jesus.

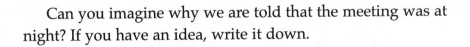

Can you imagine why we are told that the meeting was at night? If you have an idea, write it down.

I'll tell you what I think about when Nicodemus came to Jesus. I have two ideas, so I will give them to you one at a time.

#1: I think he came at night because he didn't want others to know that he was talking with Jesus about who Jesus was. Remember, Nicodemus was a religious leader himself. I am sure he thought that everyone expected him to know all about Jesus. But Nicodemus was wise enough to ask since he didn't know! But I think he was a little embarrassed, so he went at night when others couldn't see him.

#2: And I also think that Nicodemus knew that the religious leaders didn't like Jesus. So he didn't want them to know he was talking to Him. Therefore, he went under the cover of night to see Him.

2. Nicodemus is trying to understand exactly who Jesus is because he sees Jesus doing some things that are unusual. Nicodemus asks Jesus who He is by making some statements:

Nicodemus says they know Jesus is a teacher from God.

And he says they think God is with Jesus—that is the only way they can explain the miracles He is doing.

When Nicodemus says "they" know, I think he is talking about the religious leaders.

Now Jesus responds to Nicodemus in verse 3 and tells him something that Nicodemus cannot understand. What does Jesus tell him?

3. Look at verse 4 to see what Nicodemus says back to Jesus. Write out his response.

4. Jesus knows Nicodemus is confused. Jesus has just told him that he has to be born again, and Nicodemus does not know how to be born a second time!

Look at verse 5 and write down how Jesus tells Nicodemus to be born a second time. You will see that Jesus agrees with him that we must all be born "of water"—and He is talking here about when you are born from your mother. But what other kind of birth does He mention? He tells him he must be born of what?

5. Then Nicodemus asks in verse 9, "How can these things be?" And Jesus answers him in verses 16-17—I think you may know one of these verses already! Write out John 3:16 below.

How to Become a Follower

6. You see several amazing treasures in John 3:16-17, don't you? Let's take a moment to examine them, and then we'll be finished digging for the day!

• How many people does Jesus say that God loves? Write your answer and remember one of the main reasons we are on this dig as you write it!

• How does Jesus say God feels about the world?

• Who does Jesus say God gave in order for the world to have eternal life? As you write your answer, think about who that is. Do you know? Write His name.

You are right! Jesus is talking about Himself. Remember Dig Two when we unearthed who Jesus was and why He came? Now you see again why Jesus came as He talks to Nicodemus!

Think again now about how in Dig Two we talked about Adam and Eve dying spiritually? Well, Jesus is talking about the same idea with Nicodemus. Jesus tells him that we are all born physically but that in order to live forever—in heaven with God and Jesus—we have to be born a second time—spiritually.

And I bet you remember that we also talked in Dig Two about the fact that when God told Adam and Eve they would die if they ate the fruit that He was talking about spiritual death. And because they disobeyed and ate, they did die spiritually. And so did all of their children for all time. So we needed someone to give us a way to be born again—born a second time—spiritually. And here you see Jesus and Nicodemus talking about this too!

What kind of life do you receive if you believe in Jesus? Look in verse 16 again.

Do you know what *eternal* means? If you don't, look it up in a dictionary and get your mom or dad to talk about the definition with you. Write the definition below.

• What does Jesus tell Nicodemus he will need to do in order to have eternal life?

- What will you need to do in order to have eternal life?

Nicodemus was very wise to find Jesus and talk with Him. When he did, Jesus found a way to talk about the most important topic of all—eternal life! Nicodemus was brave enough to ask the question—a very important question: How can this be?

And because Nicodemus asked the question and Jesus answered it, we have a very clear answer to how we are to be born a second time—and why we are to be born a second time.

Have you been born again? Ask your mom or dad to talk with you about salvation—being born again—and eternal life. I know that they'd really like to!

And I am going to take a break from all of our hard digging and enjoy a snack! What about you?

LAYER THREE: He Knows Everything!

Wow, have you rested up from layers one and two? That was really hard work, but look what you know now about Nicodemus—and about eternal life!

Today you will meet a woman whom Jesus went out of His way to meet. And you will see how Jesus knew all about her—even though He had never met her before! Amazing!

1. Read John 4:3-30, 40-42 below. It is a long section, but it is a great story. Take your time and really think as you read so you can answer the questions that follow.

3He left Judea and went away again into Galilee. **4**And He had to pass through Samaria. **5**So He came to a city of Samaria called Sychar, near the parcel of ground that Jacob gave to his son Joseph; **6**and Jacob's well was there. So Jesus, being wearied from His journey, was sitting thus by the well. It was about the sixth hour. **7**There came a woman of Samaria to draw water. Jesus said to her, "Give Me a drink." **8**For His disciples had gone away into the city to buy food. **9**Therefore the Samaritan woman said to Him, "How is it that You, being a Jew, ask me for a drink since I am a Samaritan woman?" (For Jews have no dealings with Samaritans.) **10**Jesus answered and said to her, "If you knew the gift of God, and who it is who says to you, 'Give Me a drink,' you would have asked Him, and He would have given you living water." **11**She said to Him, "Sir, You have nothing to draw with and the well is deep; where then do You get that living water? **12**"You are not greater than our father Jacob, are You, who gave us the well, and drank of it himself and his sons and his cattle?" **13**Jesus answered and said to her, "Everyone who drinks of this water will thirst again; **14**but whoever drinks of the water that I will give him shall never

thirst; but the water that I will give him will become in him a well of water springing up to eternal life."
15The woman said to Him, "Sir, give me this water, so I will not be thirsty nor come all the way here to draw." **16**He said to her, "Go, call your husband and come here." **17**The woman answered and said, "I have no husband." Jesus said to her, "You have correctly said, 'I have no husband'; **18**for you have had five husbands, and the one whom you now have is not your husband; this you have said truly." **19**The woman said to Him, "Sir, I perceive that You are a prophet. **20**"Our fathers worshiped in this mountain, and you *people* say that in Jerusalem is the place where men ought to worship." **21**Jesus said to her, "Woman, believe Me, an hour is coming when neither in this mountain nor in Jerusalem will you worship the Father. **22**"You worship what you do not know; we worship what we know, for salvation is from the Jews. **23**"But an hour is coming, and now is, when the true worshipers will worship the Father in spirit and truth; for such people the Father seeks to be His worshipers. **24**"God is spirit, and those who worship Him must worship in spirit and truth." **25**The woman said to Him, "I know that Messiah is coming (He who is called Christ); when that One comes, He will declare all things to us."
26Jesus said to her, "I who speak to you am *He.*"

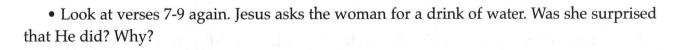

27At this point His disciples came, and they were amazed that He had been speaking with a woman, yet no one said, "What do You seek?" or, "Why do You speak with her?" **28**So the woman left her waterpot, and went into the city and said to the men, **29**"Come, see a man who told me all the things that I *have* done; this is not the Christ, is it?" **30**They went out of the city, and were coming to Him.

40So when the Samaritans came to Jesus, they were asking Him to stay with them; and He stayed there two days. **41**Many more believed because of His word; **42**and they were saying to the woman, "It is no longer because of what you said that we believe, for we have heard for ourselves and know that this One is indeed the Savior of the world."

• Look at verses 7-9 again. Jesus asks the woman for a drink of water. Was she surprised that He did? Why?

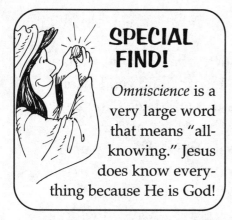

SPECIAL FIND!

Omniscience is a very large word that means "all-knowing." Jesus does know everything because He is God!

• Jesus says something in verse 14 that should remind you of part of the story of Nicodemus. What kind of life does Jesus tell the woman He can give her?

Again, we see Jesus talking with someone about eternal life—the most important thing anyone can tell someone else about!

This time He talks about "living water" too, and we will talk about this term in a later dig.

Now Jesus wants to help the woman really understand who He is, so He asks her about her husband. When she answers, she says she doesn't have one. And Jesus then says, "That is right, but you have had five husbands before. And you are living with a man now who is not your husband!"

How did Jesus know this? Because He knows everything and everyone. We cannot hide from Him! And He asks this woman about her husband because He wants her to know she does not need to hide.

When the woman understands who Jesus is, what does she do? Look again at verses 28-29 and write it below.

• Because the woman did not try to hide any longer, she told everyone what had happened! What did the people do? Read verse 30 and verses 40-41 and write what you find. I'll get you started.

v. 30: they went out of the city and were _____ _____ _____

v. 40: They were asking Him _____ _____ _____ _____

v. 41: Many more _____.

• Read verse 42 again and write what the people said to the woman about Jesus.

Isn't it amazing to see how Jesus talked to this woman in a way that she knew she did not have to be afraid? She knew she did not have to hide from Him! And then she was so excited about what He did for her, she told everyone else!

Let's look at two more things before we stop digging. We aren't to the bottom of this layer yet!

Read verses 9 and 27. Do you see that it was unusual for Jesus, a Jewish man, to talk with a Samaritan woman? Remember, though, that Jesus came to earth for all people!

We need to remember than even though people are different from us, Jesus loves them! Now, one last valuable treasure and we'll be at the bottom! Read verse 3 again.

• Now look back at the map on page 59 and see if you think Jesus had to go through Sychar to get from Judea to Galilee. What do you think?

Do you think that this verse could mean that Jesus knew the woman would be at the well and He wanted to go there to talk with her? I do! I think He wanted to go to Samaria to tell the woman about eternal life!

Remember, Jesus will always go out of the way to help us understand truth! And remember that because He knows everything, He knows all about you! Aren't you glad?

SPECIAL FIND! The Samaritans were people who lived in Samaria, a district next to Judea and Galilee. The Jews did not like the Samaritans, who were foreigners.

2. While you are looking at locations, turn to Encounters with Jesus on pages 18-19 and circle the town this woman lived in. Our verses mentioned Samaria, which is the region where the town of Sychar was. The meeting was in Sychar. Also color this part of the drawing.

Super! You made it to the bottom! You've done a great job! Have a glass of milk and some cookies...or popcorn and juice!

LAYER FOUR: Faith Is the Key

You are surely digging out some awesome treasures. I hope you are beginning to see how valuable they are—and I hope you are excited about them!

Today, you will meet another woman Jesus was pleased with. This woman was so confused and her life was so sinful that everyone knew she was a sinner. The Bible even calls her a sinner! Jesus was excited because she chose to take a chance and believe that He was the Son of God!

Let's get started before I tell you the entire story!

1. Read the Scripture from Luke 7 below.

³⁶Now one of the Pharisees was requesting Him to dine with him, and He entered the Pharisee's house and reclined *at the table*. ³⁷And there was a woman in the city who was a sinner; and when she learned that He was reclining *at the table* in the Pharisee's house, she brought an alabaster vial of perfume, ³⁸and standing behind *Him* at His feet, weeping, she began to wet His feet with her tears, and kept wiping

them with the hair of her head, and kissing His feet and anointing them with the perfume. **39**Now when the Pharisee who had invited Him saw this, he said to himself, "If this man were a prophet He would know who and what sort of person this woman is who is touching Him, that she is a sinner."
40And Jesus answered him, "Simon, I have something to say to you." And he replied, "Say it, Teacher." **41**"A moneylender had two debtors: one owed five hundred denarii, and the other fifty. **42**"When they were unable to repay, he graciously forgave them both. So which of them will love him more?" **43**Simon answered and said, "I suppose the one whom he forgave more." And He said to him, "You have judged correctly." **44**Turning toward the woman, He said to Simon, "Do you see this woman? I entered your house; you gave Me no water for My feet, but she has wet My feet with her tears and wiped them with her hair. **45**"You gave Me no kiss; but she, since the time I came in, has not ceased to kiss My feet. **46**"You did not anoint My head with oil, but she anointed My feet with perfume. **47**"For this reason I say to you, her sins, which are many, have been forgiven, for she loved much; but he who is forgiven little, loves little." **48**Then He said to her, "Your sins have been forgiven." **49**Those who were reclining *at the table* with Him began to say to themselves, "Who is this *man* who even forgives sins?" **50**And He said to the woman, "Your faith has saved you; go in peace."

2. Where was Jesus when He met this woman? Verse 37 tells you.

3. Describe what happens when the woman comes in to the house where Jesus is.

4. Read verse 39 again. Was the man who had invited Jesus to dinner surprised that Jesus let the woman near Him?

5. What does Jesus say about the woman when His host questions Him about her? Look in verses 44-47 to see. Write what you think.

6. Now look at verse 48 and verse 50 to see what Jesus said to the woman. Write your answer. Be sure to note two main things He said.

How to Become a Follower

7. What did Jesus say saved the woman?

8. Look back to Layer One where you were digging in the story of Nicodemus (page 55) and see again what Jesus told him he had to do to be saved—to have eternal life.

9. What does it mean to believe? Is it the same as having faith? Do you know? Let's look at another verse that talks about faith. Read Hebrews 11:6 below.

⁶And without faith it is impossible to please *Him*, for he who comes to God must believe that He is, and *that* He is a rewarder of those who seek Him.

What do you learn about faith?

You see again, don't you, that faith and believing are the same? To have faith in Jesus, you must believe that He is the Son of God and that He came to earth to save you from sin! We'll keep talking about this, but think about faith and believing today. And ask yourself if you have believed in Jesus.

I'm off to ride my bike. What about you?

LAYER FIVE: The Most Important Thing

It is hard for me to believe that we are almost to the bottom of Dig Four! Time is really passing by since I am having so much fun with you!

Don't you like meeting some of the men and women Jesus talked to while He was on earth? Isn't it awesome to see how He spoke to each one in a different way and how He loved each one even though they were different? A confused religious leader. A woman who felt like she needed to hide the truth. A woman who was well known as a sinner.

But He loved them all, and they were all special to Him.

Well, today you will meet another man and read a very sad story. It is a story about a man who was a ruler who wanted to meet Jesus because of all he was hearing about Him. And he, too, wanted to know how to get eternal life! But the story is sad because of how it ends. Let's read it together so you can see what I mean.

Truth Trackers: Jesus Our Savior and Friend

1. Below is Luke 18:18-30. Read these verses and then answer the questions that follow.

18A ruler questioned Him, saying, "Good Teacher, what shall I do to inherit eternal life?" **19**And Jesus said to him, "Why do you call Me good? No one is good except God alone. **20**"You know the commandments, 'DO NOT COMMIT ADULTERY, DO NOT MURDER, DO NOT STEAL, DO NOT BEAR FALSE WITNESS, HONOR YOUR FATHER AND MOTHER.'" **21**And he said, "All these things I have kept from *my* youth." **22**When Jesus heard *this*, He said to him, "One thing you still lack; sell all that you possess and distribute it to the poor, and you shall have treasure in heaven; and come, follow Me." **23**But when he had heard these things, he became very sad, for he was extremely rich. **24**And Jesus looked at him and said, "How hard it is for those who are wealthy to enter the kingdom of God! **25**"For it is easier for a camel to go through the eye of a needle than for a rich man to enter the kingdom of God." **26**They who heard it said, "Then who can be saved?" **27**But He said, "The things that are impossible with people are possible with God." **28**Peter said, "Behold, we have left our own *homes* and followed You." **29**And He said to them, "Truly I say to you, there is no one who has left house or wife or brothers or parents or children, for the sake of the kingdom of God, **30**who will not receive many times as much at this time and in the age to come, eternal life."

• What is the question the man asks in verse 18?

Again, we see someone ask the very important question about eternal life!

• Jesus responds differently to this man than He responded to others. We keep seeing that Jesus talks to each person in a way that will help them. This time He talks to the man about the commandments. And what does the man say in verse 21?

• Then Jesus gives the man His answer. What is it? Read verse 22. What does Jesus tell the young man to do?

• How does the man respond? Look at verse 23. How did the young man feel?

• Why did the man respond this way?

How to Become a Follower

- Jesus then says it is hard for someone who is very rich to enter heaven. Can you think of why? Write any idea you may have, even if you are not sure if it is really correct.

I think that people who have a lot of money and possessions may feel like they have everything. Sometimes, I think that they may wonder if they need God. But if they come to see that they do need Him, like this man we read about, then they need to be willing to let God do what He knows is best with their lives—and sometimes they think that He may make them give all of their wealth away.

I think Jesus told this man to give his money and things away just so the man could see for himself that these things were still more important to him than Jesus was.

One important lesson to learn from this sad story is that *nothing* is ever more important than knowing Jesus and being His friend. You must learn not to let anything or anyone come between you and Jesus and between you and God.

I hope you have enjoyed this dig. I have because I like knowing more about how Jesus met people different from Him and talked to them about the most important question of life—eternal life.

You know, I live in the desert of the Middle East, and we eat different food from people who live in France. Today when I stopped for lunch I heard a boy ask the waiter if he could order escargot.

The waiter did not know what the boy wanted! I knew because I have been to France. But I didn't eat escargot when I was there because I couldn't think of eating snails! Yeah, snails!

I went over to the boy's table and introduced myself and told him that we don't eat escargot in Israel. But I asked him if he liked falafel. He didn't know what that was! I showed him, and we had a great, fun lunch of falafel and fries!

You see being different isn't weird. It is just different. It can be really fun sometimes too! So, my new friend and I are off for an adventure in the Old City. Hope you will have your own adventure today too. And I'll see you in Dig Five!

As you think about people you know, I am sure you can think of people who are very different from you. See if you can find ways in the next week or so to talk with them and to get to know more about them. Remember, Jesus loves them!

You have had a busy dig! But hasn't it been great to meet some of the people Jesus talked to one-on-one and to see how special He treated each one? I hope that the treasures you take away from this dig will be some you will look at again and again—until you really understand what they are all about. Don't forget to record three of them below! And don't forget to "bury the treasure"!

I will look forward to the next dig. It is going to be awesome!!!

Hey! You also have a great puzzle on page 67.

Truth Trackers: Jesus Our Savior and Friend

Truth Treasures for the Week

1.

2.

3.

Bury the Treasure:

For God so loved the world, that He gave His only begotten Son, that whoever believes in Him should not perish, but have eternal life (John 3:16).

How to Become a Follower

Name That Disciple!

Unscramble the names of the twelve men who followed Jesus. Once you've unscrambled their names, use the numbers to find out what these men became. See if you can remember the names of these important men that we studied on the last dig. It will be a good review to see if your "remembery" is working!

Scrambled Name	Unscrambled Name
1. H O J N	_ _ _ _ 3
2. S E A M J	_ _ _ _ _ 17 2
3. E R T E P	_ _ _ _ _ 13 9
4. W R E D A N	_ _ _ _ _ _ 15 4
5. P I H L I P	_ _ _ _ _ _ 12
6. W E M L O O H T R A B	_ _ _ _ _ _ _ _ _ _ _ 5 6 14
7. T T H E W A M	_ _ _ _ _ _ _ 7
8. H O M A S T	_ _ _ _ _ _ 8 18
9. S M E A J	_ _ _ _ _ 16 10
10. A S D U J	_ _ _ _ _
11. D A E U S A D H T	_ _ _ _ _ _ _ _ 11 19
12. M O N I S	_ _ _ _ _ 20 1

_ _ _   _ _ _   _ _ _ _ _ _ _ _ _   _ _ _ _ _
1 2 3   4 5 6   7 8 9 10 11 12 13 14 15   16 17 18 19 20

solution on page 195

Dig 5

The Puzzle of Parables

Tools of the Trade

1. Colored pencils
2. Pen or pencil
3. Dictionary
4. The Parables of Jesus on pages 82-83
5. Key Words game on page 84

Directions for Diggers

I have missed digging with you. Glad you're back and ready to go! Hop in and let's get going.

In the last dig you will remember that you saw how Jesus talked with a person when He was alone with them. In this week's dig, we are going to begin to look at some of the things Jesus taught large groups of people.

This dig will be fun because you can see the difference in the way Jesus talks with crowds compared to the one-on-one conversations He had. You will see how exciting it is to hear what Jesus says and to try and understand what He means in the stories He tells.

Don't forget to check in with headquarters!

Truth Trackers: Jesus Our Savior and Friend

LAYER ONE: Stories That Tell Us the Truth

When Jesus taught groups of people, He often told stories that are called *parables*. A parable is a special kind of story that teaches a lesson. Usually a parable will tell you something by comparing one thing to something else. When we know what the things in a parable stand for, we can understand what the parable is teaching.

At one point, Jesus' disciples asked Him why He spoke to the people in parables. Let's see what He says in response to their question.

1. Read Matthew 13:10-13, 16-17 below and see what Jesus' disciples asked.

10And the disciples came and said to Him, "Why do You speak to them in parables?" **11**Jesus answered them, "To you it has been granted to know the mysteries of the kingdom of heaven, but to them it has not been granted. **12**"For whoever has, to him *more* shall be given, and he will have an abundance; but whoever does not have, even what he has shall be taken away from him. **13**"Therefore I speak to them in parables; because while seeing they do not see, and while hearing they do not hear, nor do they understand.
16"But blessed are your eyes, because they see; and your ears, because they hear. **17**"For truly I say to you that many prophets and righteous men desired to see what you see, and did not see *it*, and to hear what you hear, and did not hear *it*.

• What do the disciples ask in verse 10?

• Write out verse 11 below to see what Jesus says back to the disciples.

• What does Jesus say in verse 13 about why He uses parables to teach?

2. It may be hard to understand what He says in verses 12-13, but I think He is saying that some people will believe in Him and that they will understand the parables. These people will be blessed with abundance.

Others are not going to believe that He is the Son of God and that He has come to be the Savior of the world, and so they will not be able to understand the parables. Jesus says these are the people who will not be blessed but will have things taken away.

3. So we see that the parables are stories that teach truth. These stories are an interesting way to help people see what God wants them to do, to see how He wants them to live.

Tomorrow, we will begin to look at some of the parables and see how Jesus taught. And we will see if we can understand the stories and learn the lessons He was teaching when He told the parable. It will be fun!

I hope you have something fun planned for the rest of your day! I am going to read a great book that I have almost finished! See you next layer!

LAYER TWO: Lost and Found

In Layers Two and Three, we are going to look at three short parables that all teach the same lesson. And we are going to see why He told these parables on this day when He spoke to the crowds. You'll be excited when you see how Jesus used parables.

1. Read Luke 15:1-3 to see who was in the crowd on the day Jesus told the three parables we are studying today.

¹Now all the tax collectors and the sinners were coming near Him to listen to Him. ²Both the Pharisees and the scribes *began* to grumble, saying, "This man receives sinners and eats with them." ³So He told them this parable…

• Who was in the crowd?

• Why were the people in the crowd grumbling?

• Do you remember who the Pharisees were? You saw information about them in Dig Three and in Dig Four. Go back to Dig Three, Layer Five, to the "Special Find" box on page 49 if you need help in remembering. Write who the Pharisees were below.

Scribes were the men responsible for copying the Scriptures onto parchment so that there were more copies for people to use. There were no printing presses or copy machines or computers, so these men had a BIG job. And since they were copying God's Word, every letter had to be copied exactly. Every punctuation mark had to be copied perfectly. Can you image how careful they had to be in their work?

But also think about how much time they spent reading the Word of God! They were reading and copying the Scriptures for hours and hours almost every day!

Are you surprised that *these* men were grumbling that Jesus was spending time with men who were called sinners? Wouldn't you think men who spent their lives copying the Word of God would be excited that people were getting to know Jesus?

• Again, note that you see tax gathers included with the sinners. Who was the tax collector that Jesus asked to go with Him and help Him in His work? Think hard! If you can't remember, go back to Dig 3, Layer 5 and look again at number 2.

2. Now let's read the first parable Jesus tells the Pharisees and scribes. It is short, so it will not take long to read it. As you read, think about why Jesus may have told *this* parable to these men.

³So He told them this parable, saying, ⁴"What man among you, if he has a hundred sheep and has lost one of them, does not leave the ninety-nine in the open pasture and go after the one which is lost until he finds it? ⁵"When he has found it, he lays it on his shoulders, rejoicing. ⁶"And when he comes home, he calls together his friends and his neighbors, saying to them, 'Rejoice with me, for I have found my sheep which was lost!' ⁷"I tell you that in the same way, there will be *more* joy in heaven over one sinner who repents than over ninety-nine righteous persons who need no repentance." (Luke 15:3-7)

• What is lost in this story?

• How many sheep are not lost?

• Does the man worry about the one lost sheep? What does he do?

• Is he excited when he finds his sheep?

• When Jesus finishes telling the story, He compares the story to what happens in heaven. When He makes the comparison in verse 7, who is everyone in heaven rejoicing over?

• How many people are they rejoicing over?

• Now think about the story Jesus told. What in the story stands for the one sinner who repented?

So do you see how the story about the lost sheep was told to help them think about a person who was lost and needed to know Jesus? When the sheep was found, the man who owned it was happy. When the sinner who was lost repented, all of heaven rejoiced! Do you see how the story was about something that was lost but how Jesus was teaching about sinners and God's love?

Don't forget this parable because we are going to talk more about it and the lesson it teaches. And we will talk about why Jesus told it to the Pharisees and scribes.

3. Now let's read the next short parable that He tells this same group of people on the same day. Read the parable below.

SPECIAL FIND!
The word *repent* means to change your mind about something.

⁸"Or what woman, if she has ten silver coins and loses one coin, does not light a lamp and sweep the house and search carefully until she finds it? ⁹"When she has found it, she calls together her friends and neighbors, saying, 'Rejoice with me, for I have found the coin which I had lost!' ¹⁰"In the same way, I tell you, there is joy in the presence of the angels of God over one sinner who repents." (Luke 15:8-10)

• What is lost in this story?

• What does the woman do to find it?

• What does she do when she finds it?

• What does Jesus compare the lost coin to in the story. Look at verse 10 again to see.

• Who is happy when the sinner repents?

4. Now look at the drawing The Parables of Jesus on pages 82-83 and find the two parables you read about today. Circle these and look carefully at the drawing to see if you are reminded of what you have dug up! Take time to color these two sections of the drawing.

That is all of the digging we will do today. It is time to take a break. In Layer Three, we will look at the last parable Jesus told this group on this day. It is the story of a lost boy!

You are doing well. I am rejoicing today over you and the fact that you are discovering so many treasures! See you in Layer Three. In the meantime, have some fun!

LAYER THREE: A Wayward Son

Okay, here we go! We are going to complete our study of the three parables that teach the same lesson.

Remember that Jesus told these stories to a group of Pharisees and scribes who were upset that He was spending time with sinners and tax collectors. And remember that the first story was about a lost sheep and the second about a lost coin.

Ready? Let's go!

1. Read Luke 15:11-32. Take your time and read carefully since this story is longer than the other two.

11And He said, "A man had two sons. **12**The younger of them said to his father, 'Father, give me the share of the estate that falls to me.' So he divided his wealth between them. **13**"And not many days later, the younger son gathered everything together and went on a journey into a distant country, and there he squandered his estate with loose living. **14**"Now when he had spent everything, a severe famine occurred in that country, and he began to be impoverished. **15**"So he went and hired himself out to one of the citizens of that country, and he sent him into his fields to feed swine. **16**"And he would have gladly filled his stomach with the pods that the swine were eating, and no one was giving *anything* to him. **17**"But when he came to his senses, he said, 'How many of my father's hired men have more than enough bread, but I am dying here with hunger! **18**'I will get up and go to my father, and will say to him, "Father, I have sinned against heaven, and in your sight; **19**I am no longer worthy to be called your son; make me as one of your hired men."' **20**"So he got up and came to his father. But while he was still a long way off, his father saw him and felt compassion *for him*, and ran and embraced him and kissed him. **21**"And the son said to him, 'Father, I have

The Puzzle of Parables

sinned against heaven and in your sight; I am no longer worthy to be called your son.' **22**"But the father said to his slaves, 'Quickly bring out the best robe and put it on him, and put a ring on his hand and sandals on his feet; **23**and bring the fattened calf, kill it, and let us eat and celebrate; **24**for this son of mine was dead and has come to life again; he was lost and has been found.' And they began to celebrate.
25"Now his older son was in the field, and when he came and approached the house, he heard music and dancing. **26**"And he summoned one of the servants and *began* inquiring what these things could be. **27**"And he said to him, 'Your brother has come, and your father has killed the fattened calf because he has received him back safe and sound.' **28**"But he became angry and was not willing to go in; and his father came out and *began* pleading with him. **29**"But he answered and said to his father, 'Look! For so many years I have been serving you and I have never neglected a command of yours; and *yet* you have never given me a young goat, so that I might celebrate with my friends; **30**but when this son of yours came, who has devoured your wealth with prostitutes, you killed the fattened calf for him.' **31**"And he said to him, 'Son, you have always been with me, and all that is mine is yours. **32**'But we had to celebrate and rejoice, for this brother of yours was dead and *has begun* to live, and *was* lost and has been found.'"

I bet you have heard this story before! It is about one young son who took his part of his father's money and left home. He did not use the money wisely. When he ran out of money and was unhappy with the way he was living, he returned to his father.

His father was so happy to see him that he threw a party to welcome him home. His father said it was like the young son had been dead and was now alive.

The older son who had worked hard and stayed home was upset with the father. But what did the father say to him? Look in verses 31-32.

2. Does this story remind you of the story of the lost sheep and lost coin?

3. Yes, in all three stories something was lost and found. And when it was found, there was much happiness. But in two stories something was *not* lost and had always been there: in the first story, it was 99 sheep; in the last story, it was an older son.
How do you think you would have felt if you had been the older son?

4. Now let's think together about why Jesus told these stories to the men that day.

75

Truth Trackers: Jesus Our Savior and Friend

Remember they were religious men. So we would think that they would be happy that men who were sinners were spending time with Jesus. Why do you think they were upset first of all?

Yes, I think they were upset because they did not think a man who was a great teacher of truth should be with sinners.

5. So why do you think Jesus told these stories to men who thought in that way?

Me too. I think He wanted them to see that what isn't lost doesn't need to be found! The 99 sheep were not lost and neither was the older son. So they did not need to be found. Jesus wanted them to see that sinners need to be found! And He wanted them to see that the fact that sinners are lost is the very reason He would spend time with them! Remember why Jesus came to earth? Saving people from sin was His job!

Do you ever wish you could avoid people who are not very nice? Who seem to be mean or stuck up? Talk to your mom and dad about this lesson and see if they can help you think of ways you can be a friend to others who need a friend—in the same way that Jesus did!

I am very pleased that you have worked so hard to understand parables and to look at these three very important ones!

6. Look again at The Parables of Jesus on pages 82-83 and circle the parable you read about today. Color this part of the drawing!

Now after you finish with the chart, take a moment and write in a few short sentences the lesson Jesus was teaching by telling the three parables you have just dug through.

_____

LESSON OF THE PARABLES OF LOST THINGS:

_____

See you in Layer Four! You're great!

The Puzzle of Parables

LAYER FOUR: Building Your House

Today you will continue looking at Jesus' teaching in the form of parables. You will look at one short parable that He told to a multitude (a large group of people). I hope you are having a good time looking at the teachings of Jesus. There are so many great treasures in these stories to dig out! Let's dig!

1. Look first at the verse below to see who comes to Jesus to hear His stories and learn from Him on this.

¹When Jesus saw the crowds, He went up on the mountain; and after He sat down, His disciples came to Him. (Matthew 5:1)

2. Where did Jesus go to teach this large group of people?

3. Jesus talks for a long time to these people. We are not going to read all He says because it would take too long. So we are going all the way to Matthew 7:24-27 and look at the next parable you will study.

²⁴"Therefore everyone who hears these words of Mine and acts on them, may be compared to a wise man who built his house on the rock. ²⁵"And the rain fell, and the floods came, and the winds blew and slammed against that house; and *yet* it did not fall, for it had been founded on the rock. ²⁶"Everyone who hears these words of Mine and does not act on them, will be like a foolish man who built his house on the sand. ²⁷"The rain fell, and the floods came, and the winds blew and slammed against that house; and it fell—and great was its fall."

• Let's talk our way through the story. Look at verse 24 again. What kind of man is this part of the story about?

• What does this wise man do?

• What happened to the house when the storm came?

Truth Trackers: Jesus Our Savior and Friend

• Now let's look at the second part of the story. Read verse 26 and see what kind of man Jesus talks about now.

• What does this man do?

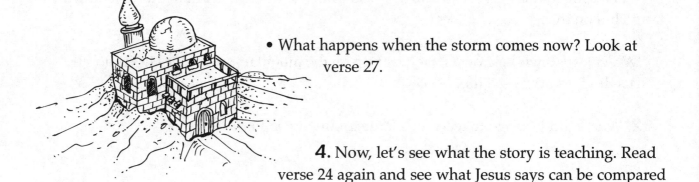

• What happens when the storm comes now? Look at verse 27.

4. Now, let's see what the story is teaching. Read verse 24 again and see what Jesus says can be compared to the wise man.

5. Look at verse 26 and see what Jesus compares to the foolish man.

Can you see that this story about men and how they build their houses is teaching about people and how they act when they hear the Word of God? If you are wise, you act upon what Jesus says to do by doing it. If you are foolish, you do **not** do what Jesus says!

Parables are fun, aren't they? Are you catching on to how the parable is a story about something that really teaches a truth about something else? I'll bet you are!

6. Circle this parable on the drawing on pages 82-83 and color that portion of the drawing.

7. Now, one last question: Which kind of person are you? Wise or foolish? Are you going to do what you are learning about the Word of God? I hope so!

**See you in Layer Five. I can't believe we are that far into this dig.
I am having so much fun that I feel like we just started digging!
Take a fun break!**

The Puzzle of Parables

LAYER FIVE: Never, Ever, Ever, Ever Give Up!

Before you start today, grab a dictionary if you don't already have it with you. You'll need it almost right away.

I am excited that you have almost completed Dig Five! You are getting to be a professional digger! So let's see what you can unearth today!

Remember to check in with headquarters.

1. Read Luke 11:1,5-10. This is such a great parable. I know you will really like it! It teaches an awesome lesson too.

¹It happened that while Jesus was praying in a certain place, after He had finished, one of His disciples said to Him, "Lord, teach us to pray just as John also taught his disciples."

⁵Then He said to them, "Suppose one of you has a friend, and goes to him at midnight and says to him, 'Friend, lend me three loaves; ⁶for a friend of mine has come to me from a journey, and I have nothing to set before him'; ⁷and from inside he answers and says, 'Do not bother me; the door has already been shut and my children and I are in bed; I cannot get up and give you *anything.*' ⁸"I tell you, even though he will not get up and give him *anything* because he is his friend, yet because of his persistence he will get up and give him as much as he needs.

⁹"So I say to you, ask, and it will be given to you; seek, and you will find; knock, and it will be opened to you. ¹⁰"For everyone who asks, receives; and he who seeks, finds; and to him who knocks, it will be opened."

- Who is talking to Jesus in verse 1?

- What does he ask Jesus to teach them about?

- What time does the man go to his friend's house to borrow bread? Look at verse 5 to see.

- Does the friend give the man the bread at first?

SPECIAL FIND!

Jesus chose 12 men to be with Him and to work with Him. These men are called disciples, and they are also called apostles.

Anyone who followed Jesus and wanted to learn what He taught and follow Him were called disciples. The word *disciple* means "student" or "learner." None of this larger group of people were called apostles.

Truth Trackers: Jesus Our Savior and Friend

Right. The friend tells the man who wants to borrow bread to go away. He says that it is too late to get up and give him bread because his family is already asleep.

• But read verse 8 and see why the friend finally gives the man the bread he asks for.

• Do you know what *persistence* means? If not, use the dictionary and look it up. Write out a definition.

PERSISTENCE!!

2. Okay, now let's think through what Jesus is teaching. First, remember what the disciple had asked Jesus to teach them. What was it? You'll dig out the answer in verse 1.

3. Now look at verses 9 and read what Jesus says about asking, seeking, knocking. I'll help you list what He says:

_____ and it will be given unto you

_____ and you will find

_____ and it will be opened to you

4. Now see what He says in verse 10. I'll help you again.

Everyone who asks _____

He who seeks _____

To him who knocks, it will be _____

80

The Puzzle of Parables

So don't you think Jesus is telling us to ask, to seek, to knock when we pray? If we don't receive what we ask for, we should keep seeking an answer. If we don't see what God is saying when we seek, we should keep knocking.

Remember that the man who was persistent—who kept on asking—was given the bread!

Are you persistent when you pray? Remember that God wants us to keep asking! When we are persistent in prayer, God will answer according to His will.

5. Take one moment to circle and color this parable on The Parables of Jesus on pages 82-83.

6. Don't forget your work below—and your puzzle on page 84.

This has been a fun dig, don't you think? I like parables because they are a little like riddles. They make you think and think, but when you see what the story means you have a great treasure.

We will look at some other parables next dig and see what else we can learn about Jesus' teaching. I will look forward to digging with you again soon!

Truth Treasures for the Week

1.

2.

3.

Bury the Treasure:

The Lord is my rock and my fortress and my deliverer, my God, my rock, in whom I take refuge (Psalm 18:2).

The Parables of Jesus

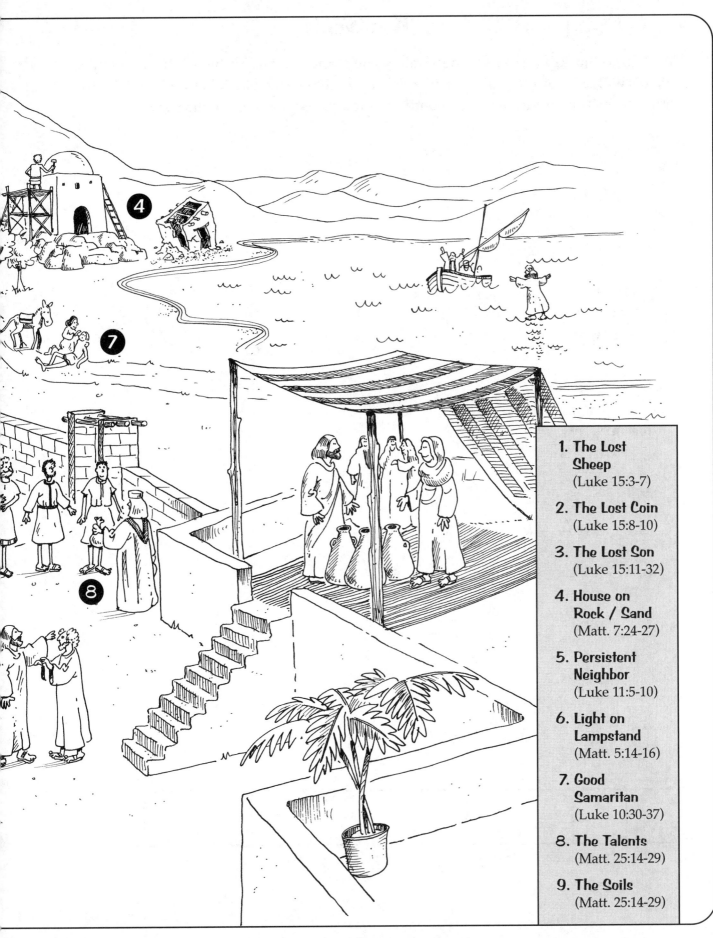

1. **The Lost Sheep** (Luke 15:3-7)
2. **The Lost Coin** (Luke 15:8-10)
3. **The Lost Son** (Luke 15:11-32)
4. **House on Rock / Sand** (Matt. 7:24-27)
5. **Persistent Neighbor** (Luke 11:5-10)
6. **Light on Lampstand** (Matt. 5:14-16)
7. **Good Samaritan** (Luke 10:30-37)
8. **The Talents** (Matt. 25:14-29)
9. **The Soils** (Matt. 25:14-29)

Truth Trackers

Key Words

To find this key phrase that describes some of the parables we've studied, fill in the blanks with the correct missing letters. After you fill in each blank in numbers 1-12, then transfer those letters to the corresponding numbered squares in the diagram.

1. _ I G H T

2. C _ I N

3. _ H E E P

4. R E P E N _

5. F _ T H E R

6. C L A Y T O _

7. _ I G

8. _ O L L O W E R

9. S _ N

10. B _ I L D

11. S I N _ E R

12. S A N _

1	2	3	4	5	6	7	8	9	10	11	12

solution on page 195

Dig 6

Tracking Truth in Parables

Tools of the Trade

1. Colored pencils
2. Pen or pencil
3. The Parables of Jesus on pages 82-83
4. Connect the Dots to Truth on page 98

Directions for Diggers

This will be another exciting dig since you will be reading more parables and looking for what Jesus was teaching as He told each one of these stories!

I am eager to get started, are you? It is so much fun to look at the way Jesus taught and to know that we can understand what many religious leaders of His day struggled to understand!

Ready? Let's go!!!

LAYER ONE: Let Your Light Shine

Do you remember the parables you worked though in Dig Five? Yes, you read the stories about lost things: a lost sheep, a lost coin, and a young man who was lost to

his family. Also, you read about men who built houses on rock and sand. Then, you ended with the story of a man who was persistent in his request for bread. Do you remember what *persistence* means?

Okay, good job. Now, just one more question: Why did Jesus teach by telling parables? If you can't remember, look back and see what we talked about last week in Layer One of Dig Five on pages 70-71.

Good. Now that you have in your mind the parables we have dug through together and you remember the way parables are told and why, let's look at a new one!

1. Read Matthew 5:1 again, and then read Matthew 5:14-16.

1When Jesus saw the crowds, He went up on the mountain; and after He sat down, His disciples came to Him.
14"You are the light of the world. A city set on a hill cannot be hidden; **15**"nor does *anyone* light a lamp and put it under a basket, but on the lampstand, and it gives light to all who are in the house. **16**"Let your light shine before men in such a way that they may see your good works, and glorify your Father who is in heaven."

You read Matthew 5:1 in the last dig, when you were digging through the parable of the men who built houses on rock and sand. We mentioned that Jesus talked for a long time to this group of people. Now we are going to look at something else He talked to the group about.

You just read what He said in verses 14-16 above.

- What does Jesus tell the people they are?

- What does Jesus say cannot be hidden?

Next, in verse 15, He talks about lighting a lamp and not hiding it. He says men do not put it under a peck measure—that is a basket. So He is saying that men do not light a lamp and hide it under a basket. That would be pointless, wouldn't it?

- What does He say they do with it? Look in verse 15 again.

- Yes, He says men put the lamp on a lampstand. What does the lamp do?

- How does Jesus end the parable? What does He tell the people to do?

Jesus encourages the people to live in a way that others can see that they love Jesus and obey Him. He tells them not to hide the fact that they love God and Jesus. He says that others will want to glorify God when they see how people who love the Lord live!

Do you act like you love Jesus? Do you do the things He asks you to do—like obey your parents? Like being kind to other guys and girls in your school? Like talking to the boy or girl other kids won't talk to or hang out with?

Think about whether you are hiding your light or whether your light is on display for all to see! Think about whether or not you live in a way that people see that you love the Lord. Remember, if you do, Jesus said that it would be like a city on a hill whose light could not be hidden. In the dark of night, if you are in the valley you can see clearly the light from the city up on the hill! And if you love the Lord and obey Him, people can see clearly that He is in your life!

2. Turn to the drawing The Parables of Jesus on pages 82-83 and color this parable.

Great dig! I'll catch you in Layer Two!

LAYER TWO: Questions Uncover Truth

Today we will prepare to dig through another parable that Jesus told to the people He was teaching. We will see what happens just before Jesus tells the parable. It has been fun to try and understand how Jesus taught, hasn't it?

Let's get started so we are ready to look at the parable itself by Layer Three.

1. Read Luke 10:23-29 to see who Jesus is talking to when He tells the story we will dig through today.

²³And turning to the disciples, He said privately, "Blessed *are* the eyes which see the things you see, ²⁴for I say to you, that many prophets and kings wished to see the things which you see, and did not see *them*, and to hear the things which you hear, and did not hear *them*." ²⁵And behold, a certain lawyer stood up and put Him to the test, saying, "Teacher, what shall I do to inherit eternal life?" ²⁶And He said to him, "What is written in the Law? How does it read to you?" ²⁷And he answered and said, "YOU SHALL LOVE THE LORD YOUR GOD WITH ALL YOUR HEART, AND WITH ALL YOUR SOUL, AND WITH ALL YOUR STRENGTH, AND WITH ALL YOUR MIND; AND YOUR NEIGHBOR AS YOURSELF." ²⁸And He said to him, "You have answered correctly; DO THIS, AND YOU WILL LIVE." ²⁹But wishing to justify himself, he said to Jesus, "And who is my neighbor?"

• In verse 23, you will see who Jesus is talking to. Who is it?

• In verse 25, you see one person asks Jesus a hard question. Who asks the question?

• In verse 25, what question did the man ask Jesus?

• Jesus answers the man by asking him a question. He asks the lawyer what is written in the Law. When Jesus asks this question, He is asking the man what the Old Testament says that could answer the question. The man answers Jesus in verse 27. Write it out below.

• Does the lawyer answer correctly? Look at verse 28 to see what Jesus says.

• The lawyer asks one more question. Verse 29 says he asked the question to *justify* himself. Justifying himself means that he was looking for a reason that he could use as an excuse not to have to love everyone! What is the question the man asks to justify himself? Look in verse 29 and write it below.

Now to answer the man's question, Jesus tells the parable we want to dig through. But before we dig through the parable, we will take a break and begin fresh tomorrow. I think you've done some hard digging to get to this point, and I want you to be ready to really think when we look at the parable called "The Good Samaritan"!

LAYER THREE: The Most Famous Parable

Today we will dig through the parable that Jesus is going to tell the group of people we studied about yesterday. The parable we are going to work on today is probably Jesus' most famous parable. Can you tell me what it is called? Yes, "The Good Samaritan"! It is a story that asks a very important question. Let's see if we can dig out that important question!

Remember that Jesus is talking to His disciples. And remember to think about the man—the lawyer—who asked Jesus the question.

Tracking Truth in Parables

1. Read the parable as Luke recorded it.

30 Jesus replied and said, "A man was going down from Jerusalem to Jericho, and fell among robbers, and they stripped him and beat him, and went away leaving him half dead. **31** "And by chance a priest was going down on that road, and when he saw him, he passed by on the other side. **32** "Likewise a Levite also, when he came to the place and saw him, passed by on the other side. **33** "But a Samaritan, who was on a journey, came upon him; and when he saw him, he felt compassion, **34** and came to him and bandaged up his wounds, pouring oil and wine on *them*; and he put him on his own beast, and brought him to an inn and took care of him. **35** "On the next day he took out two denarii and gave them to the innkeeper and said, 'Take care of him; and whatever more you spend, when I return I will repay you.' **36** "Which of these three do you think proved to be a neighbor to the man who fell into the robbers' *hands*?" **37** And he said, "The one who showed mercy toward him." Then Jesus said to him, "Go and do the same." (Luke 10:30-37)

• What happened to the man who was going from Jerusalem to Jericho? Verse 30 tells you.

• What did the robbers do to the man?

• Read verses 31-33 again and let's list the people who passed this man and see what each did. I'll help a little!

PEOPLE: **WHAT THEY DID:**

1 a _____   passed ____ ____ ____ _____ side

2 a _____   _____ ____ ____ ____ _____ side

3 a _____   ____ _____ compassion

• Let's write out the six things the Samaritan did for the man on the day he found him. Read verse 34 again and I'll keep helping you.

1 ____ ____ him

2 _____ ____ ____ wounds

3 pouring ____ ____ ____ __ ____

4 put ____ __ ____ ____ ____

5 brought ____ __ ____ inn

6 ____ ____ __ him

89

Truth Trackers: Jesus Our Savior and Friend

• Now look in verse 35 to see what this Samaritan did for the man on the next day. Again, let's make notes. I think writing out something important helps to remember it!

1 took out _____ _____ and gave them to ___ _____

2 and said, _____ _____ ___ _____

3 and whatever _____ _____ _____ when I return, ___ _____ _____ _____

Amazing, isn't it! He was willing to take care of the expense of caring for the man—even if it was going to cost more! He said to do what needed to be done and if it cost more, he'd pay next time he came to the inn! He didn't just take care of one night's expense. He was willing to take care of the expense until the man was better!

• When Jesus completes the story, what does He do? Right. He asks another question—remember He and the lawyer you read about yesterday keep asking questions back and forth! Write out the question Jesus asks now from verse 36.

• Now look in verse 37 to see how the lawyer responded. Remember that the whole conversation started because he was trying to justify the fact that he did not have to love everyone! Look back to Layer Three if you need to see this again. How did the lawyer answer in verse 37?

• And then what did Jesus say to the lawyer in verse 37?

Isn't this an amazing story! Can you see why it is Jesus' most famous parable? At the beginning of this layer, I mentioned to you that the parable asked a very important question. Do you know what the question is? If you do, write it below.

Well, the question is "Who is my neighbor?" The lawyer did not want to be willing to love everyone. And when Jesus told him to follow the commandment that he had quoted, it said to love your neighbor as yourself! So the man wanted to know who his neighbor was! And Jesus sure gives him an awesome answer, doesn't He? The neighbor was the man who needed help. Your neighbor is anyone in need!

2. Turn again today to the drawing The Parables of Jesus on pages 82-83 and color this parable.

Tracking Truth in Parables

What do you think? Who is your neighbor? Can you write what you think below? Be sure to explain who your neighbor is and note how you think you should treat your neighbor.

LAYER FOUR: Using Your Gifts for Jesus

Today our parable is a story about a man who gave money to his servants. You will be surprised, I think, to see what happens in the story. But when you think hard and understand the meaning of the story, I think you will see why it makes perfect sense.

Let's dig!

1. First, before you read the story, look at Matthew 24:3 and see who asked Jesus a question.

3As He was sitting on the Mount of Olives, the disciples came to Him privately, saying, "Tell us, when will these things happen, and what *will be* the sign of Your coming, and of the end of the age?"

So we see that some of His disciples have asked Him a question about the end of time and Jesus' return to earth. He talks for a long time, and like before we are going to just look at part of what He says by reading our parable.

2. Now, read our story below. Take your time since it is a little long.

14"For *it is* just like a man *about* to go on a journey, who called his own slaves and entrusted his possessions to them. **15**"To one he gave five talents, to another, two, and to another, one, each according to his own ability; and he went on his journey. **16**"Immediately the one who had received the five talents went and traded with them, and gained five more talents. **17**"In the same manner the one who *had received* the two *talents* gained two more. **18**"But he who received the one *talent* went away, and dug *a hole* in the ground and hid his master's money.
19"Now after a long time the master of those slaves came and settled accounts with them. **20**"The one who had received the five talents came up and brought five more talents, saying, 'Master, you entrusted five talents to me. See, I have gained five more talents.' **21**"His master said to him, 'Well done, good and faithful slave. You were faithful with a few things, I will put you in charge of many things; enter into the joy of your master.'

> **SPECIAL FIND!**
>
> A *talent* was a denomination of money like a ten-dollar bill is ten one dollars.
>
> But a talent was worth about $1000!

Truth Trackers: Jesus Our Savior and Friend

22"Also the one who *had received* the two talents came up and said, 'Master, you entrusted two talents to me. See, I have gained two more talents.' 23"His master said to him, 'Well done, good and faithful slave. You were faithful with a few things, I will put you in charge of many things; enter into the joy of your master.' 24"And the one also who had received the one talent came up and said, 'Master, I knew you to be a hard man, reaping where you did not sow and gathering where you scattered no *seed*. 25'And I was afraid, and went away and hid your talent in the ground. See, you have what is yours.' 26"But his master answered and said to him, 'You wicked, lazy slave, you knew that I reap where I did not sow and gather where I scattered no *seed*. 27'Then you ought to have put my money in the bank, and on my arrival I would have received my *money* back with interest. 28'Therefore take away the talent from him, and give it to the one who has the ten talents.' 29"For to everyone who has, *more* shall be given, and he will have an abundance; but from the one who does not have, even what he does have shall be taken away." (Matthew 25:14-29)

• When the man gets ready to go on his journey, he gives his servants money. Look in verse 15 and list what he gives to each one. Note what you find below.

one = _____ talents

to another = _____ talents

to another = _____ talents

• Verse 15 says how the man decided on the amount of money to give to each servant. How did he decide? What was his decision "according" to?

• Read verses 16-18 and write below what each man did with his money.

5 talents =

2 talents =

1 talent =

Tracking Truth in Parables

• Read verses 20-21 and see what happened to the man who had five talents when the master returned. What did the master say to him?

• The man who had two talents also did well. Write what the master said to him. Review their conversation in verses 22-23.

• Let's see what happened to the man who had one talent. Read verses 24-25 and see what the man says to the master. Why does he say he hid the talent?

• Can you see in these same verses why the man was afraid of the master?

• See what the master said the man should have done with the money in verse 27.

• The master knew that if the money had been in the bank it would have been safe and he would have made some money in interest. What does the master say to do with the talent in verse 28?

• Write out the end of the parable to help you see what the lesson is. The end is in verse 29.

Does this verse remind you of something else you have dug through? Yes, in Dig Five, Layer One (on pages 70-71) we looked at why Jesus said He taught in parables. He talked about people who were blessed with abundance being people who believe in Him. And He said that they would understand the parables.

He also talked about others who are not going to believe that He is the Son of God and that He has come to be the Savior of the world. He said that they will not be able to understand the parables. Jesus said these are the people who have things taken away from them.

Now we see Him talk again about people who have much getting more—the talent. And He also talks about the one who does not have very much having to give up the talent.

I know this lesson may be a little difficult to follow, but think about how the parable started. The man was giving the talents according to the gifts or abilities he felt each man had. He will give the most money to the man he felt had the greatest gifts and abilities.

So you need to think about the fact that what you have been given is to be used wisely. It is a gift from God. Some have gifts that make them good artists, some are athletic and are good at sports, some are creative and are good cooks. What are you good at? The lesson is that you are to use your gifts and abilities to the maximum. If you do, God will give you more!

Do you use the gifts and abilities God has given you? Maybe you can talk with your parents about what they see as your greatest gift or ability. I bet they would really like to talk with you about that, and I know they can help you see how to use this to the maximum!

3. Before you stop for the day, turn to the drawing The Parables of Jesus on pages 82-83 and color this parable.

LAYER FIVE: What Will Grow in Your Heart?

Today we will look at one last parable. I want you to dig through this parable because it has such a great lesson in it!

1. Look in Luke 8:4 to see who Jesus is going to be telling this parable to. Where were these people from?

⁴And when a great multitude were coming together, and those from the various cities were journeying to Him, He spoke by way of a parable.

SPECIAL FIND!

Farmers in the first century didn't use machines to sow their fields with seed. They took handfuls of seed and, with a sweeping motion, threw the seed on the ground they had plowed with a hand plow pulled by an animal. A skillful sower could spread grain seeds very evenly.

2. Read Luke 8:5-8, 11-15 and think carefully about the kinds of ground the seeds are sown on.

⁵"The sower went out to sow his seed; and as he sowed some fell beside the road; and it was trampled under foot, and the birds of the air ate it up.
⁶"And other *seed* fell on rocky *soil*, and as soon as it grew up, it withered away, because it had no moisture.
⁷"An other *seed* fell among the thorns; and the thorns grew up with it, and choked it out."
⁸"And other *seed* fell into the good soil, and grew up, and

Tracking Truth in Parables

produced a crop a hundred times as great." As He said these things, He would call out, "He who has ears to hear, let him hear."

11"Now the parable is this: the seed is the word of God. **12**"And those beside the road are those who have heard; then the devil comes and takes away the word from their heart, so that they may not believe and be saved. **13**"And those on the rocky *soil are* those who, when they hear, receive the word with joy; and these have no *firm* root; they believe for a while, and in time of temptation fall away. **14**"And the *seed* which fell among the thorns, these are the ones who have heard, and as they go on their way they are choked with worries and riches and pleasures of *this* life, and bring no fruit to maturity. **15**"And the *seed* in the good soil, these are the ones who have heard the word in an honest and good heart, and hold it fast, and bear fruit with perseverance."

• Now using the chart that follows, list what kind of soil the seeds were sown on. Then write what happened to the seeds on each kind of soil.

TYPE OF SOIL   WHAT HAPPENED TO THE SEED

verse 5

verse 6

verse 7

verse 8

• Now let's see what Jesus says about the parable. First look in verse 11 to see what He says the seed stands for. Write it down.

The disciples didn't understand the parable, so Jesus explained it in verses 12-15. We need to think together! You'll have to dig through these verses with me and see what we can learn about how each group responds. Just like the disciples had to when Jesus told the story to them!

I'll list for you who each group is, and then you go back to each verse and complete the chart by writing out what happens to the word.

Truth Trackers: Jesus Our Savior and Friend

WHO EACH GROUP IS   WHAT HAPPENS TO THE WORD THAT IS SOWN

verse 12 Those beside the road are those who have heard...then

verse 13 Those on rocky soil are those who hear, receive the word with joy, and have no firm root.

verse 14 The seeds among the thorns are the ones who have heard and as they go on their way they are choked with cares.

verse 15 The seed in good soil are ones who have heard the word in an honest and good heart, and hold it fast.

So do you see how different people respond differently to the Word of God being given to them? How have you responded to the Word of God that you have heard? How are you responding to what you are learning in our digs? Think about it and tell God that you want to respond correctly!

3. For the last time in this dig, turn to the drawing The Parables of Jesus on pages 82-83 and color this parable.

4. Now note your truth treasures, bury your treasure, and check out the great puzzle on page 98.

I am very, very proud of you! You have worked so hard to dig through eight parables, and I know you have learned amazing lessons! I

96

surely hope that you are going to be wise like the man who built his house on the rock and obey what you are learning!

See you at the next dig. Can you believe it will be Dig Seven? Awesome! Let's get some exercise for our bodies since our brains have been stretched!

Truth Treasures for the Week

1.

2.

3.

Bury the Treasure:

You shall love the Lord your God with all your heart, and with all your soul, and with all your strength, and with all you mind; and your neighbor as yourself (Luke 10:27).

Truth Trackers

Connect the Dots to Truth

In Luke 10:27, Jesus says to "love your neighbor as yourself." But first Jesus tells us to:

Love the Lord your God...

with all your

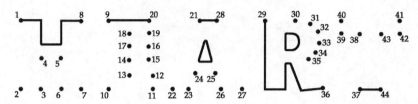

with all your

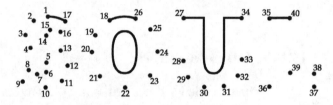

with all your

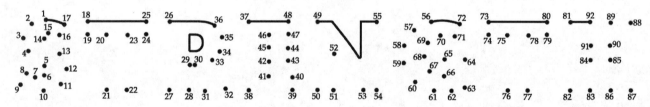

with all your

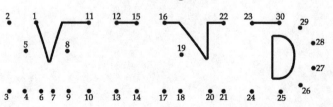

solution on page 196

Dig 7

Jesus the Miracle Worker

Tools of the Trade

1. Colored pencils
2. Pen or pencil
3. The Miracles of Jesus on page 110-111
4. The Timeline of the Life of Christ on pages 191-192
5. The Secret of Miracles on page 112

Directions for Diggers

Wasn't it amazing to look at some of the parables Jesus told and understand why He told them? I hope you learned as much as I did! And I hope you were challenged to live like Jesus taught the people to live!

We are going to go on two digs now that will uncover some of the miracles Jesus performed. We will also discover why He performed miracles or signs, and we will see what happened to people who heard about what He was doing!

We will unearth some awesome treasures, too, that will help us to see the things on this earth that Jesus has power over! Do you remember a big word—*omniscience*—that you saw in Dig Four? Well, in this dig you will see another big word that looks a little like omniscience. Watch for it because it gives you a great treasure about Jesus.

As you work through this dig, think about why Jesus came to earth. These miracles helped Him accomplish His goal. You'll see how as you dig.

Well, I've talked enough. I know you are rarin' to go, so let's head out!

Truth Trackers: Jesus Our Savior and Friend

LAYER ONE: It Takes a Lot of Power

As I said, in this dig we will discover signs and miracles that Jesus performed and also discover why He did them. In order to keep you from getting too tired and in order to focus on some of the most memorable miracles, we are going to dig in only one gospel—the Gospel of John.

1. There is a verse at the end of John's gospel that tells us why he wrote this book. Let's start digging at this verse. Read John 20:30-31 below and see what you can uncover.

30Therefore many other signs Jesus also performed in the presence of the disciples, which are not written in this book; **31**but these have been written so that you may believe that Jesus is the Christ, the Son of God; and that believing you may have life in His name.

• Why does John say he wrote this gospel that is full of Jesus' signs and miracles?

• Does John say that he included all of the miracles Jesus performed?

Signs and Miracles!!!

• How many other miracles did Jesus do according to John?

• Who does he say was there when Jesus did these miracles?

2. Jesus also says that the signs He performed got people's attention and made them believe that He was the Son of God. Dig through John 4:48 and see what Jesus said about signs and miracles. (He calls miracles *wonders* in this verse.)

Write what Jesus says after you read this verse.

48So Jesus said to him, "Unless you *people* see signs and wonders, you *simply* will not believe."

that you might believe!

100

Jesus the Miracle Worker

3. You have noticed that I keep saying "signs and miracles" when I talk about these awesome things Jesus did. And we just saw Him call them *wonders*. So let me explain to you that the word *sign* really means *attesting miracle*.

So, do you know what attesting means? You know what I am going to ask you to do, don't you? Yes, look up *attest* and write the definition.

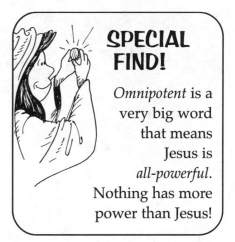

SPECIAL FIND!

Omnipotent is a very big word that means Jesus is *all-powerful*. Nothing has more power than Jesus!

4. So you see now that the signs we are talking about were really the miracles themselves. And they revealed who Jesus was. The fact that He could do these wonders was like saying, "Yes, He is God! He has awesome power and control over all kinds of things!" They were a way that people could know He had awesome power and could do anything—because He was God, the Son of God.

Are you excited about seeing Jesus' power in action?! You should be because He is most awesome. Think of the most powerful thing or person you know and think way, way beyond that power. You still aren't even close to His power!
Awesome! Awesome! Awesome!

Jesus is the most awesome and powerful person who ever lived—or ever will live!
Isn't it cool to worship the most powerful person in all of creation?
In fact, He created creation!

Meet you in Layer Two soon! Have a good break!

LAYER TWO: A Mother's Request

Okay, this is an exciting layer to dig through because we get to unearth facts about the first miracle Jesus ever performed. Ready! Great.

1. Read about this miracle in John 2:1-11 below. Then we'll talk about it.

¹On the third day there was a wedding in Cana of Galilee, and the mother of Jesus was there; ²and both Jesus and His disciples were invited to the wedding. ³When the wine ran out, the mother of Jesus said˙ to Him, "They have no wine." ⁴And Jesus said˙ to her, "Woman, what does that have to do with us? My hour has not yet come." ⁵His mother said˙ to the servants, "Whatever He says to you, do it." ⁶Now there were six stone waterpots set there for the Jewish custom of purification, containing twenty or thirty gallons each. ⁷Jesus said˙ to them, "Fill the waterpots with water." So they filled them up to the brim. ⁸And He said˙ to them, "Draw *some* out now and take it to the headwaiter." So they took it *to him*. ⁹When the headwaiter tasted the water which had

Truth Trackers: Jesus Our Savior and Friend

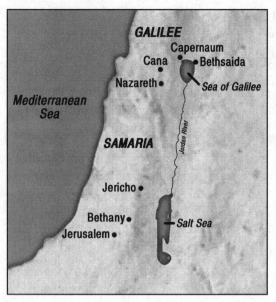

become wine, and did not know where it came from (but the servants who had drawn the water knew), the headwaiter called* the bridegroom, **10**and said* to him, "Every man serves the good wine first, and when *the people* have drunk freely, *then he serves* the poorer *wine; but* you have kept the good wine until now." **11**This beginning of *His* signs Jesus did in Cana of Galilee, and manifested His glory, and His disciples believed in Him.

• Jesus is in Cana of Galilee. This little town is not very far from Nazareth where Jesus grew up. You can see how close it is on the map. What event is Jesus attending?

• What did they run out of at the wedding?

You may not realize this, but running out of wine at a wedding could be very embarrassing to the people giving the wedding and to the man and woman being married. Think of how you might feel if your parents told you that you could have a sleep-over and they told you to tell everyone that they should plan on having pizza and ice cream when they arrived—then your dad forgot to buy the pizza and your mom forgot to pick up the ice cream! And instead of going out to get this food, they said, "It will be okay. We found some tuna and crackers in the cupboard. And we have rice cakes with peanut butter for dessert." Wouldn't you be bummed out? Well, this is how the host would feel about running out of wine!

Jesus' mother knew how embarrassing this problem could be, and she felt sorry for these people. But Mary knew that she could go to her Son for help. She knew He had the power to do something about the mess.

• What does Jesus do?

• After Jesus tells the servants to fill the jugs with water and they pour some, they take this wine to the headwaiter. Why is he surprised by the wine? Look in verse 10 to see what he says to the bridegroom. Write what you find about the wine Jesus made from the water.

Jesus the Miracle Worker

So Jesus didn't just turn water to wine. He turned water into very **good** wine!

• Write out verse 11 below so we can talk about the result of the sign in the lives of people.

• How do you know this was the first sign or miracle? Look carefully at what verse 11 says.

Yes, the word "beginning" is our clue. Beginning means the first!

• Who does it say believed as a result?

Do you remember that we talked earlier about the fact that anyone who followed Jesus was called a disciple? So these people who believed were probably not the 12 but other men and women who were traveling with Jesus and wanting to understand who He really was. This sign convinced them!

2. One last thing to think about. The miracle that Jesus did showed that He had the power over something. Can you think of what it showed power over? It is a little hard, I think, since we have not talked about this before. But try to think and write your idea if you have one.

I think the fact that Jesus could turn water into wine showed that He had power over nature. He took one thing that nature gives us and turned it into something else that man makes from the grapes that nature gives us!

You will see as we continue to look at miracles that He has power over all kinds of things. And you will understand His power more and more as we continue to look at His miracles.

Would you have believed that Jesus had the power to turn water into wine if you had been at the wedding? Many believed that He was the Son of God after He turned the water to wine. Would you have believed then? Do you believe today that Jesus is the Son of God? Talk to your mom or dad tonight about what you are thinking about Jesus at this point.

3. Turn to the drawing The Miracles of Jesus on pages 110-111 and color this miracle you just dug through. Also notice the place where this miracle was done. Circle the location.

4. Now turn to your Timeline of the Life of Christ on pages 191-192 and check off the event you just uncovered.

You've done a great job! Hope you are eager to see the next miracle in Layer Three! See you there soon.

Truth Trackers: Jesus Our Savior and Friend

LAYER THREE: A Little Boy Is Healed

Today we are going to see another amazing miracle that Jesus did. As you read about this miracle, think about what it shows His power over and see if you can figure it out. Let's go!

1. Read this story in John 4:46-54 of a father who was very eager to see Jesus. His son was dying!

46Therefore He came again to Cana of Galilee where He had made the water wine. And there was a royal official whose son was sick at Capernaum. **47**When he heard that Jesus had come out of Judea into Galilee, he went to Him and was imploring *Him* to come down and heal his son; for he was at the point of death. **48**So Jesus said to him, "Unless you *people* see signs and wonders, you *simply* will not believe." **49**The royal official said˙ to Him, "Sir, come down before my child dies." **50**Jesus said˙ to him, "Go; your son lives." The man believed the word that Jesus spoke to him and started off. **51**As he was now going down, *his* slaves met him, saying that his son was living. **52**So he inquired of them the hour when he began to get better. Then they said to him, "Yesterday at the seventh hour the fever left him." **53**So the father knew that *it was* at that hour in which Jesus said to him, "Your son lives"; and he himself believed and his whole household. **54**This is again a second sign that Jesus performed when He had come out of Judea into Galilee.

• Where is Jesus when this man comes to Him?

• Where is the man's son? Go back to page 102 and look at the map to see how far the boy is from where Jesus is. Write the name of the city were the boy is.

• What does the man ask Jesus to do? Look in verse 49.

• Does Jesus go with the man? See what Jesus says in verse 50.

• Read verse 51 again and see what happens as the man is going home. Who comes to meet him?

Jesus the Miracle Worker

• What do the servants tell him?

• The man asks what hour of the day the boy got better. He realizes when they tell him that it was at the same time that Jesus had told him the boy would be better!

• What does verse 54 say about this miracle?

2. This miracle showed more of the power of Jesus. It was a sign! Okay, you know I am going to ask! What do you think this sign showed Jesus had power over? I think you will see if you think very hard about this story. Write what you think.

If you said "distance," I agree with you! The boy was in one town and Jesus was in another. The man asked Jesus to come to the boy. But Jesus didn't have to go! He could heal the boy at a distance!

No matter where you are, Jesus can reach you! Aren't you super glad about that?

3. We do not see anyone believe after this miracle was done. I am sure people did, but John does not tell us about them. Interesting, isn't it, that he tells us instead about someone who believed after the water was turned to wine? Can you think of who that may have been?

I think it was the royal official whose son was sick believed after the water was turned to wine. Do you know why I think that? Yes! Because he had the faith to come and ask for Jesus to heal his son! I think he had believed and he knew Jesus had the power to do anything!

So you see we didn't read about this man after the first miracle! I think that lots of people believed after every miracle. John just doesn't tell us here who they are.

4. Turn again to the drawing The Miracles of Jesus on pages 110-111 and find and color the drawing of this miracle. Look carefully at the drawing and notice where Jesus is when He performs this miracle. Think too about where the boy is He healed and see if you can find the town where He was. Notice the distance!

5. Find the Timeline of the Life of Christ on pages 191-192 and check off the event you uncovered today.

See you in Layer Four. I'm heading for a treat! What about you?

Truth Trackers: Jesus Our Savior and Friend

LAYER FOUR: Pick Up Your Mat and Walk

Incredible to see how powerful Jesus is, isn't it? I can hardly wait to dig through the next miracle, so let's get to it.

1. Read about the next miracle in John 5:1-13 and watch for what upset some people about this sign.

1After these things there was a feast of the Jews, and Jesus went up to Jerusalem. **2**Now there is in Jerusalem by the sheep *gate* a pool, which is called in Hebrew Bethesda, having five porticoes. **3**In these lay a multitude of those who were sick, blind, lame, and withered, *waiting for the moving of the waters;* **4***for an angel of the Lord went down at certain seasons into the pool and stirred up the water; whoever then first, after the stirring up of the water, stepped in was made well from whatever disease with which he was afflicted.* **5**A man was there who had been ill for thirty-eight years. **6**When Jesus saw him lying *there*, and knew that he had already been a long time *in that condition*, He said˚ to him, "Do you wish to get well?" **7**The sick man answered Him, "Sir, I have no man to put me into the pool when the water is stirred up, but while I am coming, another steps down before me." **8**Jesus said˚ to him, "Get up, pick up your pallet and walk." **9**Immediately the man became well, and picked up his pallet and *began* to walk. Now it was the Sabbath on that day. **10**So the Jews were saying to the man who was cured, "It is the Sabbath, and it is not permissible for you to carry your pallet." **11**But he answered them, "He who made me well was the one who said to me, 'Pick up your pallet and walk.'" **12**They asked him, "Who is the man who said to you, 'Pick up *your pallet* and walk'?" **13**But the man who was healed did not know who it was, for Jesus had slipped away while there was a crowd in *that* place.

• How long has this man been lame? (Lame means he couldn't walk very well.) The reason he tells Jesus he cannot get in the water first is because he can't walk.

• What would happen to the first person in the water after it was stirred? Look in verse 4.

• Who stirred the water?

• When Jesus tells the man to get up and walk, what happens? Look in verse 9.

Jesus the Miracle Worker

Look in verse 10 to see what day it was. The verse does not name a day of the week. But it says it was the Sabbath. That means it was Saturday. The Jewish people rest and worship on Saturday instead of Sunday, and they call that day the Sabbath. But some of them—the Pharisees we have talked about before—were very strict about what someone should do on this special day.

And one of the things that they did not want people to do was to carry the rug that they sat on (their pallet) while they walked. They felt like this was work, and the Bible (Old Testament) said that the Jewish people should not work on the Sabbath!

But who had told this man he could take his pallet and walk? This is the same question these Jewish leaders asked. Who was it?

Yes, Jesus told the man. Jesus understood that the rule about work on the Sabbath was not a rule that meant someone who believed in Him could not be healed on that day!

I think this man believed who Jesus was, don't you? If you look in verse 15 below, you will see that he was telling people Jesus had healed him.

15The man went away, and told the Jews that it was Jesus who had made him well.

2. Again, take a moment and think about the story. What did Jesus have power over in this story? You may say that He had power over sickness, and this is correct. But there is something else here that is a little harder to uncover. But I think it is a neat find.

Yes—time. This man had been sick for 38 years, but that did not matter when Jesus healed him! Jesus is greater than time!

3. Find the drawing The Miracles of Jesus on pages 110-111 and find the drawing of the miracle and circle the place where this miracle was done. You see that Jesus was performing miracles all over! Color the drawing if you'd like.

I hope you are thinking of how Jesus showed His power over nature, over distance, over sickness, over time. Aren't you happy to know that He is all-powerful and that nothing can stop Him when you need His help? Remember the new word you learned in Layer One? Yes, Jesus is omnipotent!

4. Find the Timeline of the Life of Christ on pages 191-192 and check off the event you uncovered today.

See you in Layer Five after you have some fun! I am learning a new, fun game called miniature golf. Someday I hope to play real golf on a big course like Tiger Woods, but for now this is a great place to learn. What new thing do you want to learn to do? Maybe you can talk to your parents about it and see if they can help you get started.

Truth Trackers: Jesus Our Savior and Friend

LAYER FIVE: Time for Review

Jesus performed seven miracles that John recorded. We have already looked at three of them in this dig. Next dig, we will finish digging through the other four. Today, I thought we could have some fun!

Take about ten or fifteen minutes and draw a picture on the next page of one of the miracles we have uncovered through this dig. I think it will be fun to think about the detail of one of these and to sketch it! Don't you?

Review the miracles:
- turning the water to wine that showed Jesus' power over nature
- the healing of the royal official's son that showed Jesus' power over distance
- the healing of the man sick for 38 years that showed Jesus' power over time and sickness!

Which one will you draw? I'll tell you in the next dig which one I am doing!

You have been very diligent, and I am very proud of you! You are learning great truths—like the fact that Jesus can always reach you and the fact that time cannot keep Him from helping you! Don't forget to thank God for all He is showing you!

And are you thinking about how these miracles helped Jesus work toward accomplishing His goal for coming to earth? We'll talk about that more next dig.

When you complete your sketch and your truth treasures, there is a fun puzzle on page 112 for you to try!

And have a good break and rest up for Dig Eight! Don't forget to bury the treasure!

TRUTH TREASURES FOR THE WEEK

1.

2.

3.

BURY THE TREASURE:

But these have been written that you may believe that Jesus is the Christ, the Son of God; and that believing you may have life in His name (John 20:31).

SKETCH OF A MIRACLE!!!

The Miracles of Jesus

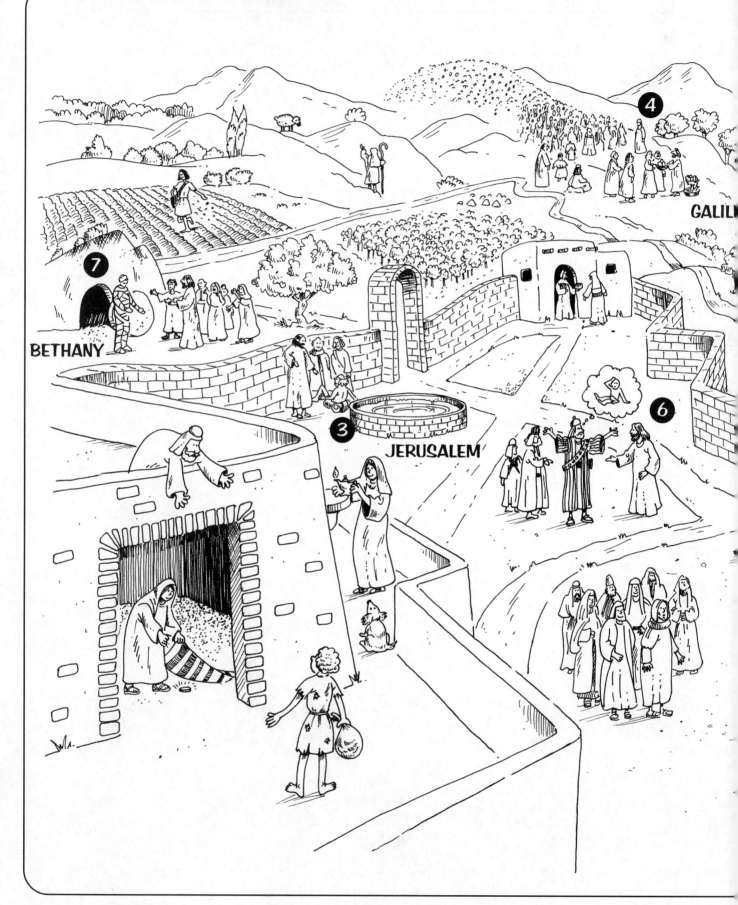

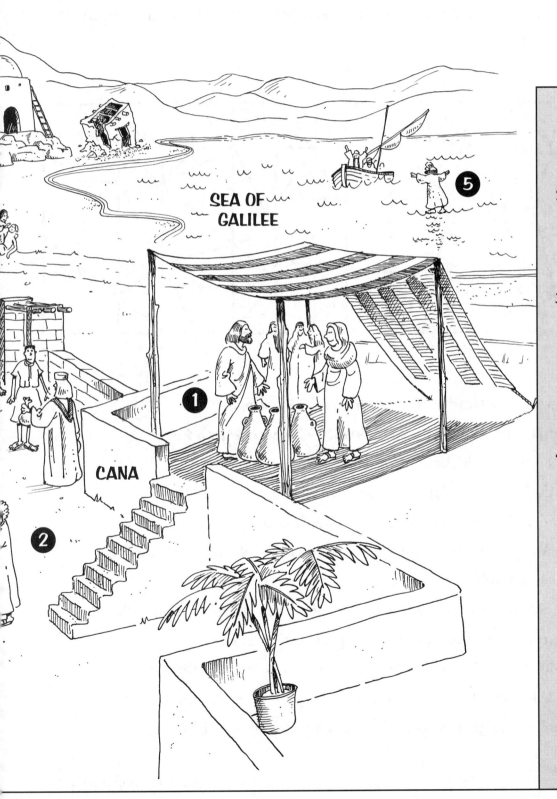

1. Jesus turns water into wine (John 2:1-11)

2. Jesus heals the Royal Official's son (John 4:46-54)

3. Jesus heals the lame man who cannot get into the pool when the water is stirred (John 5:1-13)

4. Jesus feeds over 5000 with 5 loaves and 2 fish (John 6:1-14)

5. Jesus walks on the water (John 6:16-21)

6. Jesus heals the man blind from birth (John 9:1-17)

7. Jesus raises Lazarus from the dead (John 11:1-47)

Truth Trackers

The Secret of Miracles

The Bible says this: "To please God you must believe that He is, and that He is a rewarder of those who diligently seek Him."

When we read about the miracles that Jesus performed in the New Testament, we usually read about someone in the crowd of people who were with Jesus who had something we all want. Do you know what it is? Solve the puzzle below by working through numbers 1-12 below.

Miracles require...

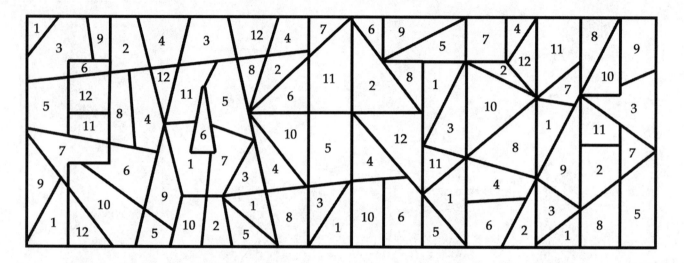

1. If Jesus is part of the Trinity, color each space with a one.
2. If Jesus couldn't turn water into wine, color each space with a two.
3. If Jesus was born in Bethlehem, color each space with a three.
4. If Jesus had 13 disciples, color each space with a four.
5. If Jesus healed a sick boy, color each space with a five.
6. If Jesus sent Mary to the store for more wine, color each space with a six.
7. If Jesus taught in parables, color each space with a seven.
8. If Jesus isn't able to save us from our sins, color each space with an eight.
9. If Jesus has power over time, color each space with a nine.
10. If Jesus couldn't make the lame man walk, color each space with a ten.
11. If Jesus was able to walk on water, color each space with an eleven.
12. If Jesus doesn't know your name, color each space with a twelve.

solution on page 196

Dig 8

Miracles, Miracles, More Miracles!

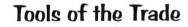

Tools of the Trade

1. Colored pencils
2. Pen or pencil
3. The Miracles of Jesus on pages 110-111
4. The Timeline of the Life of Christ on pages 191-192
5. Decode the True Message of the Miracles on page 130

Directions for Diggers

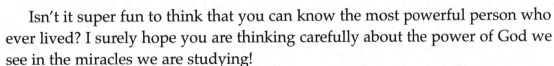

Isn't it super fun to think that you can know the most powerful person who ever lived? I surely hope you are thinking carefully about the power of God we see in the miracles we are studying!

And I hope you know that you can be Jesus' friend. In fact, He is the best friend you can ever have because He is the wisest, kindest, most loyal person who ever lived.

Jesus is awesome, and you can know Him! So let's dig though four more miracles that will give you even more of an idea of His power and greatness! And let's continue to look at how people respond when they see what He does.

Ready? Hey, wait up! Don't leave me! And don't forget to check in with headquarters!

Truth Trackers: Jesus Our Savior and Friend

LAYER ONE: Baskets and Baskets of Food

As I said, in this dig we will look at the last four miracles that John writes about in his gospel. Don't forget that John has told us that Jesus did lots of other signs and miracles. John just tells us about some of the miracles that he thought would make believers out of us! And don't forget that John tells us that this is exactly why Jesus performed miracles and why John recorded them—so that people would believe!

When you think of a sign, what do you think it does? What is the purpose of a sign? Yes! Signs either point to something or tell you something.

When you think of what John has told us about Jesus' signs, what do you think about their purpose? Right again! They too point to something. What? Oh, you are so awesome! You are right on! They pointed to the fact that Jesus was who He claimed to be—the Son of God!

So let's get to digging! We will uncover more miracles and signs and see who believed as a result of what these signs pointed to.

1. Dig through the verses below to see the story of the next miracle John tells us about. It is an amazing story!

1After these things Jesus went away to the other side of the Sea of Galilee (or Tiberias). **2**A large crowd followed Him, because they saw the signs which He was performing on those who were sick. **3**Then Jesus went up on the mountain, and there He sat down with His disciples. **4**Now the Passover, the feast of the Jews, was near. **5**Therefore Jesus, lifting up His eyes and seeing that a large crowd was coming to Him, said* to Philip, "Where are we to buy bread, so that these may eat?" **6**This He was saying to test him, for He Himself knew what He was intending to do. **7**Philip answered Him, "Two hundred denarii worth of bread is not sufficient for them, for everyone to receive a little." **8**One of His disciples, Andrew, Simon Peter's brother, said* to Him, **9**"There is a lad here who has five barley loaves and two fish, but what are these for so many people?" **10**Jesus said, "Have the people sit down." Now there was much grass in the place. So the men sat down, in number about five thousand. **11**Jesus then took the loaves, and having given thanks, He distributed to those who were seated; likewise also of the fish as much as they wanted. **12**When they were filled, He said* to His disciples, "Gather up the leftover fragments so that nothing will be lost." **13**So they gathered them up, and filled twelve baskets with fragments from the five barley loaves which were left over by those who had eaten. **14**Therefore when the people saw the sign which He had performed, they said, "This is truly the Prophet who is to come into the world." (John 6:1-14)

• Where does John tell us Jesus has gone in verse 1?

Miracles, Miracles, More Miracles!

• Who follows Him?

• Why did these people follow Jesus?

• Look at verse 5 again. Jesus already knows what He is going to do to take care of feeding these people who are coming to hear Him teach. But what does He ask Philip? (He is one of the 12 men Jesus asked to work with Him.)

• Look at verse 7 to see that Philip tried to figure out an answer that made sense. What does he say?

• In verses 8-9, another of the 12 apostles tries to help. What does Andrew say?

• Jesus does not respond to the suggestion of either man. In verse 10, what does He tell them to do?

• Then what happens in verses 11-12?

• How many baskets do they fill with the food that was left after everyone ate?

2. Look in verse 14 to see who believes as a result of this sign. Write this verse below.

3. Think hard now and see if you can tell me what this miracle showed Jesus had power over. Write what you think below.

SPECIAL FIND!

Now that's a lot of leftovers!

Some baskets that were used when Jesus lived were very large. They were large enough to hold the Apostle Paul when he was let down from the Damascus city walls (Acts 9:25)!

I think we see Jesus' power over our physical needs. Jesus knew these people would be hungry before the day was over, and He knew He had the power to meet the need of over 5,000 people!

Jesus can meet any need you have, and here He gives us a picture story of how He can meet physical needs—even if what we have looks like it isn't enough!

4. Find the drawing The Miracles of Jesus on pages 110-111 and circle the place where this miracle was done. Be sure to take the time to look at the drawing—and to color it if you'd like.

5. Now turn to your Timeline of the Life of Christ on pages 191-192 and check off the event you uncovered on this dig so far.

You are pretty awesome yourself! I love how you are hanging in there and digging with all of your might! See you in Layer Two!

LAYER TWO: Jesus Calms the Storm

Today is my favorite story about one of Jesus' miracles. I love the lesson we can learn from this one. Let's get digging!

1. Read about this miracle in John 6:16-21 below. Then we'll talk about it.

¹⁶Now when evening came, His disciples went down to the sea, ¹⁷and after getting into a boat, they *started to* cross the sea to Capernaum. It had already become dark, and Jesus had not yet come to them. ¹⁸The sea *began* to be stirred up because a strong wind was blowing. ¹⁹Then, when they had rowed about three or four miles, they saw˙ Jesus walking on the sea and drawing near to the boat; and they were frightened. ²⁰But He said˙ to them, "It is I; do not be afraid." ²¹So they were willing to receive Him into the boat, and immediately the boat was at the land to which they were going.

• Who is in the boat?

• Where are they headed?

Miracles, Miracles, More Miracles!

• What time of day is it?

• What happens to the sea after they begin to cross?

• How far had they rowed when they saw Jesus?

• Where was He when they saw Him?

• Did they expect to see Him there? What does verse 19 say about how they responded?

• What does He say to them in verse 20?

• Then in verse 21 He gets in the boat, and what happens?

Look at a verse in Matthew to see what he tells us about what happened when Jesus got into the boat. Matthew tells the same story as John, he just adds some details that John doesn't write about. Read Matthew 14:32-33.

32When they got into the boat, the wind stopped. 33And those who were in the boat worshiped Him, saying, "You are certainly God's Son!"

• What happened to the wind?

• What did the men in the boat say?

Truth Trackers: Jesus Our Savior and Friend

2. Isn't this a great story! Can you imagine being out on the water at night in a boat with a bad storm tossing you about and seeing someone walk up beside the boat on the water? One other thing Matthew tells us that John doesn't tell us is that when the men first saw Jesus coming to them on the water, they thought He was a ghost!

Who does Matthew 14:33 say believed as a result of this miracle? Right, you just wrote what they said! The men in the boat! I think it could have made me believe, don't you?

3. Now for the question you know is coming. What does this miracle show us about Jesus' power? What does He have power over?

Yes, the weather! Think about how much power it would take to stop a strong wind! Think about how much power you would need to control an earthquake! A hurricane! A tornado! He has it! And He wants you to know that His power is part of the way He will always take care of you!

Can you thank Him right now for the fact that He is powerful enough to always protect you when you call out to Him?

Sometimes when you are having a hard time or things are confusing, don't forget that Jesus can even walk on water to get to you if He has too! And think about the fact that when He got in the boat with the disciples, the storm calmed down and they were no longer afraid! Maybe you can ask Jesus to get in the boat with you when you are having a hard time or things are scary. He would really like to calm the storm for you.

4. Turn to the drawing The Miracles of Jesus on pages 110-111 and circle the place where this miracle occurred. Think about the fact that you are seeing how Jesus moved through the land of Israel as you continue to mark these miracles. It is amazing to see how far they traveled without trucks, cars, or motorbikes.

5. Find your Timeline of the Life of Christ on pages 191-192 and check off the event you dug through.

> Are you getting more excited about this God-Man called Jesus?
> I always get excited when I read the things He said and did while
> He was on the earth. But when I see how powerful He is and I think
> of the fact that He wants to know me, I get really, really excited.
> Think about that and meet me soon in Layer Three!

Miracles, Miracles, More Miracles!

LAYER THREE: Blind, and Now I See!

Today we are going to read a story that almost makes me cry because the man Jesus healed was so excited! I like it when people get excited about what Jesus does for them!

1. Let's dig through this story of a man who was blind from the day he was born and see what happens.

1As He passed by, He saw a man blind from birth. **2**And His disciples asked Him, "Rabbi, who sinned, this man or his parents, that he would be born blind?" **3**Jesus answered, "*It was* neither *that* this man sinned, nor his parents; but *it was* so that the works of God might be displayed in him. **4**"We must work the works of Him who sent Me as long as it is day; night is coming when no one can work. **5**"While I am in the world, I am the Light of the world." **6**When He had said this, He spat on the ground, and made clay of the spittle, and applied the clay to his eyes, **7**and said to him, "Go, wash in the pool of Siloam" (which is translated, Sent). So he went away and washed, and came *back* seeing. **8**Therefore the neighbors, and those who previously saw him as a beggar, were saying, "Is not this the one who used to sit and beg?" **9**Others were saying, "This is he," *still* others were saying, "No, but he is like him." He kept saying, "I am the one." **10**So they were saying to him, "How then were your eyes opened?" **11**He answered, "The man who is called Jesus made clay, and anointed my eyes, and said to me, 'Go to Siloam and wash'; so I went away and washed, and I received sight." **12**They said to him, "Where is He?" He said, "I do not know."
13They brought to the Pharisees the man who was formerly blind. **14**Now it was a Sabbath on the day when Jesus made the clay and opened his eyes. **15**Then the Pharisees also were asking him again how he received his sight. And he said to them, "He applied clay to my eyes, and I washed, and I see." **16**Therefore some of the Pharisees were saying, "This man is not from God, because He does not keep the Sabbath." But others were saying, "How can a man who is a sinner perform such signs?" And there was a division among them. **17**So they said to the blind man again, "What do you say about Him, since He opened your eyes?" And he said, "He is a prophet." (John 9:1-17)

• Do you see in verse 1 how long the man has been blind? I mentioned it already, but I want you to see how I knew!

• What question do the disciples ask Jesus in verse 2 when they pass by the man?

• What answer does Jesus give them in verse 3?

Don't you think it is awesome that Jesus says the man is not blind because he did anything wrong. He is blind so that the works of God can be seen in him when he is given his sight!

• What does Jesus do next in verses 6-7?

• Do you know why Jesus told the man to go wash in the pool? If you have an idea, write it down below.

I think Jesus had the man go wash so the man's faith could be seen. If Jesus had just healed him, the man would not have had to do anything. The blind man could have said, "Are you crazy? Do you think that rubbing mud on my eyes and telling me to wash it off is going to make me see?" But did he say that? Or did he believe enough to take a chance that what Jesus said would work?

• What happens in verse 7 after the man goes and washes in the pool?

• What do his neighbors say? John tells us several different things people were saying. Note the different things they say.

• The man keeps telling them all that he is the one! He is the one who was blind but can now see. Write out how he answers their questions about how this happened. Look in verse 11.

The people can't understand what has happened. So they take the man to the religious leaders. Remember when the religious leaders were upset when Jesus healed the lame man who was at the pool where the angel stirred the water? Can you think of why they were

Miracles, Miracles, More Miracles!

upset? If you don't remember, do back to Dig Seven, Layer Four (on pages 106-107) and read about this again.

• Read verses 14-16 again and see how the religious leaders were upset about Jesus healing this blind man for the same reason. Write below why they are upset.

• Look in verse 16 to see how upset they became! They were so upset that they said they didn't even think Jesus was from God! But some of these men said that a sinner could not perform the miracles that Jesus was doing! What does verse 16 say happened between these religious leaders because they disagreed.

The miracles and signs were getting some attention, weren't they?

• See what the blind man said about who Jesus was in verse 17. Write it below.

2. This story goes on through the end of John 9, but it is so long that we will not dig through all of it. I do want to go to the end of the story where Jesus and the man who was blind talk again and see what they say to one another. The man has been kicked out of the Temple by the religious men now because they can't understand what has happened to his eyesight. Jesus finds the man.

> ³⁵Jesus heard that they had put him out, and finding him, He said, "Do you believe in the Son of Man?" ³⁶He answered, "Who is He, Lord, that I may believe in Him?" ³⁷Jesus said to him, "You have both seen Him, and He is the one who is talking with you." ³⁸And he said, "Lord, I believe." And he worshiped Him. (John 9:35-38)

The man believes that Jesus is the Son of Man—another name Jesus called Himself.

3. Can you think of what Jesus shows His power over when He performs this miracle? When Jesus performed this miracle of healing a man who had been blind all his life, I think He shows His power over our physical bodies. Jesus can heal anything that is wrong with our bodies if it is His will to heal it!

You will need to remember that when we dug through the miracle of the man who was lame for 38 years we talked about Jesus having power over time. Jesus also healed something wrong with that man's physical body, didn't He? But because we are told how long the man had been lame, I think that is a hint that we were to look for something else. And we did, and we found it. We discovered that Jesus has power over time!

4. Turn to the drawing The Miracles of Jesus on pages 110-111 and circle the place where this miracle occurred. Look at the drawing and color it too.

5. Find your Timeline of the Life of Christ on pages 191-192 and check off the event you dug through.

You need to rest up big time for our dig tomorrow! It will take a major effort to get all the way through Layer Four. You are really going to have to dig, dig, dig! But what you will unearth will astound you! Get some rest. I surely plan to!

LAYER FOUR: A Friend Comes Back to Life!

I hope you rested up. Today is our big dig day! You will dig through the story of Jesus' most awesome miracle—at least *I* think it is the most awesome!

1. Read John 11:1-48. I know it is really long, but you won't even think of that because it is such a great story!

¹Now a certain man was sick, Lazarus of Bethany, the village of Mary and her sister Martha. ²It was the Mary who anointed the Lord with ointment, and wiped His feet with her hair, whose brother Lazarus was sick. ³So the sisters sent *word* to Him, saying, "Lord, behold, he whom You love is sick." ⁴But when Jesus heard *this*, He said, "This sickness is not to end in death, but for the glory of God, so that the Son of God may be glorified by it." ⁵Now Jesus loved Martha and her sister and Lazarus. ⁶So when He heard that he was sick, He then stayed two days *longer* in the place where He was. ⁷Then after this He said˙ to the disciples, "Let us go to Judea again." ⁸The disciples said˙ to Him, "Rabbi, the Jews were just now seeking to stone You, and are You going there again?" ⁹Jesus answered, "Are there not twelve hours in the day? If anyone walks in the day, he does not stumble, because he sees the light of this world. ¹⁰"But if anyone walks in the night, he stumbles, because the light is not in him." ¹¹This He said, and after that He said˙ to them, "Our friend Lazarus has fallen asleep; but I go, so that I may awaken him out of sleep." ¹²The disciples then said to Him, "Lord, if he has fallen asleep, he will recover." ¹³Now Jesus had spoken of his death, but they thought that He was speaking of literal sleep. ¹⁴So Jesus then said to them plainly, "Lazarus is dead, ¹⁵and I am glad for your sakes that I was not there, so that you may believe; but let us go to him." ¹⁶Therefore Thomas, who is called Didymus, said to *his* fellow disciples, "Let us also go, so that we may die with Him." ¹⁷So when Jesus came, He found that he had already been in the tomb four days. ¹⁸Now Bethany was

Miracles, Miracles, More Miracles!

near Jerusalem, about two miles off; ¹⁹and many of the Jews had come to Martha and Mary, to console them concerning *their* brother. ²⁰Martha therefore, when she heard that Jesus was coming, went to meet Him, but Mary stayed at the house. ²¹Martha then said to Jesus, "Lord, if You had been here, my brother would not have died. ²²"Even now I know that whatever You ask of God, God will give You." ²³Jesus said˙ to her, "Your brother will rise again." ²⁴Martha said˙ to Him, "I know that he will rise again in the resurrection on the last day." ²⁵Jesus said to her, "I am the resurrection and the life; he who believes in Me will live even if he dies, ²⁶and everyone who lives and believes in Me will never die. Do you believe this?" ²⁷She said˙ to Him, "Yes, Lord; I have believed that You are the Christ, the Son of God, *even* He who comes into the world."²⁸And when she had said this, she went away and called Mary her sister, saying secretly, "The Teacher is here and is calling for you." ²⁹And when she heard it, she got˙ up quickly and was coming to Him. ³⁰Now Jesus had not yet come into the village, but was still in the place where Martha met Him. ³¹Then the Jews who were with her in the house, and consoling her, when they saw that Mary got up quickly and went out, they followed her, supposing that she was going to the tomb to weep there. ³²Therefore, when Mary came where Jesus was, she saw Him, and fell at His feet, saying to Him, "Lord, if You had been here, my brother would not have died." ³³When Jesus therefore saw her weeping, and the Jews who came with her *also* weeping, He was deeply moved in spirit and was troubled, ³⁴and said, "Where have you laid him?" They said˙ to Him, "Lord, come and see." ³⁵Jesus wept. ³⁶So the Jews were saying, "See how He loved him!" ³⁷But some of them said, "Could not this man, who opened the eyes of the blind man, have kept this man also from dying?" ³⁸So Jesus, again being deeply moved within, came˙ to the tomb. Now it was a cave, and a stone was lying against it. ³⁹Jesus said˙, "Remove the stone." Martha, the sister of the deceased, said˙ to Him, "Lord, by this time there will be a stench, for he has been *dead* four days." ⁴⁰Jesus said˙ to her, "Did I not say to you that if you believe, you will see the glory of God?" ⁴¹So they removed the stone. Then Jesus raised His eyes, and said, "Father, I thank You that You have heard Me. ⁴²"I knew that You always hear Me; but because of the people standing around I said it, so that they may believe that You sent Me." ⁴³When He had said these things, He cried out with a loud voice, "Lazarus, come forth." ⁴⁴The man who had died came forth, bound hand and foot with wrappings, and his face was wrapped around with a cloth. Jesus said˙ to them, "Unbind him, and let him go." ⁴⁵Therefore many of the Jews who came to Mary, and saw what He had done, believed in Him. ⁴⁶But some of them went to the Pharisees and told them the things which Jesus had done. ⁴⁷Therefore the chief priests and the Pharisees convened a council, and were saying, "What are we doing? For this man is performing many signs." ⁴⁸If we let Him *go on* like this, all men will believe in Him, and the Romans will come and take away both our place and our nation."

Truth Trackers: Jesus Our Savior and Friend

• You see that Lazarus was sick and that his sisters sent a message to Jesus to tell Him. Look in verse 4 again and dig out what Jesus says when He gets the message. Write it below.

Do you remember another time when Jesus said that some terrible situation had happened so that the glory of God could be seen? Yes!!! The man born blind! When we see the glory of God, we see God do something that no man could do. And we realize in a new way that He is so powerful and awesome that we can never get to the bottom of who He is like we can get to the bottom of one of our digs!

• Verse 5 tells how Jesus felt about Martha, Mary, and Lazarus. What does it say?

• Verse 6 reveals something that may seem strange. If your friend was sick and his sisters asked you to come, would you do this? What did Jesus do?

SPECIAL FIND!

Tombs were cut into rock and looked like a cave.

A round stone rested in a stone track to cover the opening of the tomb.

The stone could be rolled in the track to open and close the tomb.

After the two days pass, Jesus tells His disciples that He should go to Judea. They respond with surprise because they remind Him that some Jews were trying to stone Him when He was there last time (the Pharisees you have learned about).

Jesus says that people who walk in the dark stumble. What He is saying to the disciples is that these men do not understand the truth of who He is. He says that they are walking in spiritual darkness and cannot see that He is the Son of God.

Then Jesus tells them in plain terms that Lazarus is dead. And He also tells them something else pretty amazing in verse 15. He mentions what He thinks will happen for them as a result of Lazarus' death. What does He say will happen for them?

• In verse 17, you find out how long Lazarus had been buried or been in the tomb. How long?

Miracles, Miracles, More Miracles!

• Why did Jesus wait two more days to go to His friends after He got word of Lazarus being sick? Do you remember what He said would happen as a result of what He was going to do now that Lazarus was dead?

You are awesome! Yes, He knew God would be glorified, and He knew people would believe.

Plus, He was not afraid that He could not raise Lazarus from the dead, was He? He was God, and He was all-powerful! Even stronger than death! Now, that is some kind of strong!

• Who had come to be with Martha and Mary because their brother had died? Look at verse 31 to see.

Yes, they had friends who had come to be with them. This verse tells us that "the Jews" had come to be with them. Remember that the Jews were confused about who Jesus was! Think about Nicodemus and his questions. About the rich ruler.

• What does verse 38 tell you about the grave Lazarus was buried in?

• What does Mary say to Jesus about Lazarus in verse 39? There are two things. Dig hard and uncover both! Write them below.

• Read verse 40 again. Write below what you uncover that Jesus says to Martha.

• Now look back at verses 41-42 again and search for what Jesus says to His Father, God. Let's record it. I'll help.

I thank You that You _____ _____ _____

I knew that You always _____ _____

But because of the people standing around I said it, so that they may _____ that ____ _____ ____ .

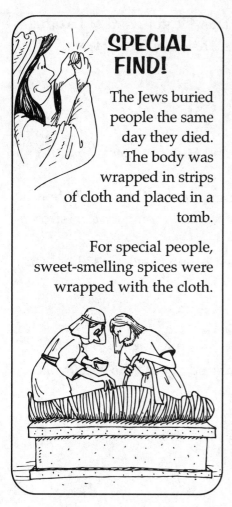

SPECIAL FIND!

The Jews buried people the same day they died. The body was wrapped in strips of cloth and placed in a tomb.

For special people, sweet-smelling spices were wrapped with the cloth.

Can you see that Jesus did not doubt that God would answer Him? Jesus says that He told Martha she would see the glory of God if she believed! And now He says that He only said this to her so that others could hear and would believe that He was God's Son when they saw the miracle He was going to do.

Again, you see that Jesus says the glory of God will be seen in the miracle.

• What happens next in verses 43-44?

• We are almost to the bottom! Hope you are hanging in there with me! Read verse 45 again now and unearth who believed as a result of the miracle. Who was it?

Isn't that exciting? Some of the people who were confused believed—just like Jesus said they would. They saw the glory of God, and they saw the Father answer His Son's prayer!

• But not all believed; what did the other Jews do? Dig in verse 46.

We meet the Pharisees again. And they are still concerned about the signs Jesus is performing! Can't you understand their concern? The signs were resulting in people believing!

• What do the Pharisees say could happen to all men if they let Jesus go on? Look at the first part of verse 48.

They were terrified that all would believe! Jesus was doing His job well!

2. Okay, I know you are really pushing, so let's finish this dig up in a hurry. First, what did Jesus show His power over?

Miracles, Miracles, More Miracles!

Yes—death! Awesome or what?! Even death is not more powerful than Jesus!

3. Turn to the drawing The Miracles of Jesus on pages 110-111 and find the location of this miracle. Circle the location and color the art.

4. Find the Timeline of the Life of Christ on pages 191-192 and chart the event you have just uncovered.

Take a very, well-deserved break. We'll talk more in Layer Five about what we just discovered!

LAYER FIVE: Signs = Belief

I asked you to be thinking of how the signs and miracles we were going to dig through helped Jesus accomplish His mission. Have you thought about that?

Well, if you think back, you remember that Jesus came to save us from sin. And in order to save us, we have to believe that He is the Son of God! These signs sure helped people to believe, didn't they?

Think back over the signs we have seen and who believed as a result of the sign:

- water turned to wine, and the disciples believed
- the royal official's son was healed, and we think many people believed
- the man who was lame for 38 years was healed, and he believed
- Jesus fed over 5,000 people with 5 loaves and 2 fish, and many of them believed
- Jesus walked on the water, and the disciples believed
- Jesus healed the man born blind, and he believed
- Jesus raised Lazarus from the dead, and many Jews believed!

You see how the signs pointed to who Jesus was, and the result was people believed!

1. Today, since you worked so hard in Layer Four, have some fun on this last dig. Turn to page 128 and draw or illustrate the sign that you thought was the most amazing.

2. And you will find a fun puzzle to solve on page 129.

Then be sure to thank God before you end this dig for all of the awesome, incredible treasure you have uncovered. And get excited because there is still more to find!

I am going to have a fun break and will look forward to Dig Nine soon!

Truth Trackers: Jesus Our Savior and Friend

TRUTH TREASURES FOR THE WEEK

1.

2.

3.

BURY THE TREASURE:

Truly, truly, I say to you, he who believes has eternal life (John 6:47).

Miracles, Miracles, More Miracles!

SKETCH OF A MIRACLE!!!

Truth Trackers

Decode the True Message of the Miracles

Since we're on a search for buried treasure, I thought you might enjoy using an ancient alphabet developed by the Egyptians. Do you remember that Mary and Joseph took the baby Jesus to Egypt to escape from the evil King Herod?

Use this ancient alphabet to decode the reason why Jesus came to our earth and what it can mean for every person who believes in Him. Match a symbol from the Egyptian alphabet with the symbol above each blank. Then fill in each blank with the letter it represents.

Egyptian Alphabet

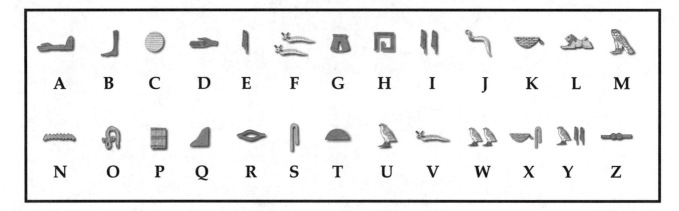

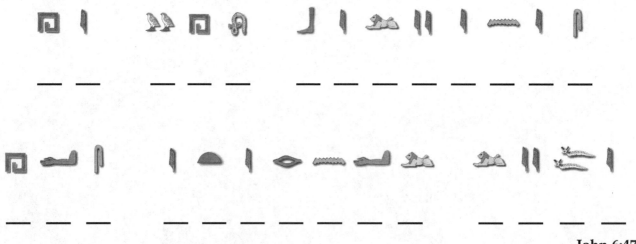

John 6:47

Draw your name, using the Egyptian alphabet:

solution on page 197

Dig 9

What's in a Name?

Tools of the Trade

1. Colored pencils
2. Pen or pencil
3. A Name Hunt on page 141

Directions for Diggers

Do you like your name? I like mine. I think it is neat. Sometimes people call me Clay for short.

A name tells us who someone is. Sometimes, it can tell you more. Sometimes it can tell you things about the person.

One of our recent presidents was named William Jefferson Clinton. Don't you think that was a big name to give a baby? People who knew him and didn't call him "Mr. President" called him Bill for short. Maybe his mom wanted him to be President of the United States one day, and she gave him a name that sounded like a president!

The man who is president when I am writing to you is named George Walker Bush. He was named George Walker because his father's name is George Herbert Bush. He was given a family name—his dad's name. When he ran for President, news reporters called him George W. so that we would know

they were talking about him and not his father. His father was also President of the United States in 1989-1992!

I know a lady who comes to the Middle East to teach people about Israel. She has a nephew whose name is Mason Caldwell. He is named Mason because his mother's last name was Mason before she married Mr. Caldwell. Mason got his name because it was a family name too—but just from his mom's family.

Mason's brother is named Lucas. Lucas got his name because his parents wanted him to have a very cool name, and he does! His aunt gave him a nickname because she likes him so much. Sometimes she calls him Lukie Luke just for fun!

People are named for lots of different reasons: They get names because their parents want them to be something special when they grow up; they get family names; they get cool names their families like; and sometimes they get names because people who like them shorten their names or give them nicknames!

In this dig, we are going to look at some of the names Jesus calls Himself. You will uncover these names and what they mean! And you will see what you can learn about Jesus from these names!

I hope you are ready, cause we are off! Don't forget to check in with headquarters!

LAYER ONE: He Meets Our Needs

You may have noticed as we have dug through verses from the Bible about the life of Christ that the men who wrote the Gospels called Jesus by names other than just Jesus. Let's see if we can think of some of them:

Only Begotten Son	The Word
Son of Man	Beloved Son
Jesus Christ	Son of God
Son of the Most High	Immanuel—God With Us

Wow! And that isn't even all of them! These are names other people called Jesus. But what we are going to do in Dig Nine is dig and find some of the names He called Himself!

We are going to dig in just one gospel—John's. In this gospel, Jesus calls Himself eight different names. In our dig, we will uncover six of these eight. Let's dig!

1. The first name we will dig to find is in chapter 6. Jesus says, "I am…" and He calls Himself something. We are searching for what He calls Himself after He says "I am." He calls Himself by this name in two different verses, and He says it in a little different way each time. But I think you will uncover it. See if you can find it. Dig!

41Therefore the Jews were grumbling about Him, because He said, "I am the bread that came down out of heaven." **42**They were saying, "Is not this Jesus, the son of Joseph, whose father and mother we know? How does He now say, 'I have come down out of heaven'?" **43**Jesus answered and said to them, "Do not grumble among

What's in a Name?

yourselves. **44**"No one can come to Me unless the Father who sent Me draws him; and I will raise him up on the last day. **45**"It is written in the prophets, 'AND THEY SHALL ALL BE TAUGHT OF GOD.' Everyone who has heard and learned from the Father, comes to Me. **46**"Not that anyone has seen the Father, except the One who is from God; He has seen the Father. **47**"Truly, truly, I say to you, he who believes has eternal life. **48**"I am the bread of life." (John 6:41-48)

Did you see the name? Great! Can you write the way He says it each time? I will give you the verses, and you record what He says each time He calls Himself by this name.

Verse 41

Verse 48

Yes, Jesus calls Himself "the bread of life."
Did you discover when you read verse 41 that the Jews were upset with Jesus again? Read verse 42 again.

You see that the Jews are confused about the fact that Jesus was saying He had come from heaven. They are talking about Him being Joseph's son. They did not believe that He was sent from God.

• In verse 44, you will uncover part of Jesus' answer to these men who are so puzzled. Look at this verse again now and see what Jesus says about people who come to Him. You should see two things. Write these below.

1:

2:

You discover that God, Jesus' Father, plays a BIG part in someone believing in Jesus, don't you? Jesus says that the Father *draws* people. This means that God puts something in people's hearts that makes them want to know Jesus and believe in Him.

Jesus also says that one day He will raise up these people who believe—and when He does they will live in heaven with Him and His Father!

• Also in talking to these men, Jesus makes a statement we have talked about before. Look in verse 47 and see who Jesus says has eternal life. Write what you see.

Jesus is talking about being "the bread of life" because He wants people to think about the fact that they need bread to live physically. If they see that they need bread to live, then He thinks they can see that they need to believe in Him in order to live spiritually.

Jesus is talking in a way that makes people think in pictures in their minds. He is talking about something they all need. And He uses something that everyone knows they must have to live. His hope is that when they think of bread and realize how important it is for physical life that they will then realize that He is important for spiritual life!

Jesus is "the bread of life." He will fill you up so that you do not have spiritual needs that are not taken care of. You need to learn to believe what He says and do what He asks you to do. When you do these things, your life will be full! Just like you have eaten lots of bread and feel full!

The next time you are really hungry and think of a great big peanut butter and jelly sandwich and how great you will feel when you eat it, think about Jesus being "the bread of life" and how good you will feel when you learn to let Him fill your needs!

You have done an awesome, awesome job! Is it time for a PBJ (peanut butter and jelly sandwich)? I think so! I got hungry talking about it. See you in Layer Two!

LAYER TWO: He Gives Us Light

Ready to dig? Me too. I know some of what we are uncovering may be a little hard to understand, but we are on a tough dig that will give us some great, great treasures if we don't stop digging!

1. Let's look at another name Jesus calls Himself in the Gospel of John. This time it is in chapter 8. See if you can find what Jesus calls Himself and write it below.

¹²Then Jesus again spoke to them, saying, "I am the Light of the world; he who follows Me will not walk in the darkness, but will have the Light of life." ¹³So the Pharisees said to Him, "You are testifying about Yourself; Your testimony is not true." ¹⁴Jesus answered and said to them, "Even if I testify about Myself, My testimony is true, for I know where I came from and where I am going; but you do not know where I come from or where I am going."

• Did you see that Jesus called Himself "the light of the world"? Who is He talking to when He says this? Look in verse 13 to see who says something to Him about what He called Himself. What group is it?

• Are you beginning to see that the Pharisees, who were a group of the Jews, are having trouble understanding who Jesus is? What do they say isn't true in verse 13?

What's in a Name?

When they say, "Your testimony is not true," they mean that what Jesus is saying about Himself is a lie. They do not believe that He is "the light of the world." They do not believe that He came from heaven.

But what does He say back to them? Yes, He says that His testimony is true! He says that they do not know where He came from or where He is going. And we know that this is correct just by what we saw in chapter 6 when He called Himself "the bread of life" and they were confused and talking about Jesus being Joseph's son!

Jesus says He is "the light of the world." Think about how dark a closet can be when you close yourself in without any light at all! Really dark, right?

Well, the world is a dark place because people are sinners. And you know all about how we became sinners. When people do not believe in Jesus, they are dead spiritually and they live in darkness—because they do not understand that Jesus came to save them.

But when Jesus came into the world, He came to give life. And when we believe in Him, we can walk in the light because we understand who He is!

Think of the darkest place you have ever been. Now think about how happy you were that you could turn a light on! Or that you had a flashlight! That is how dark the world is. And Jesus came to turn on the light! He is the light of the whole world!

Jesus wants to turn on the light for you too. If you do not understand who He really is and why He really came, ask Him to turn on the light for you! He will!

You should talk to your mom or dad about Jesus being "the light of the world" so that they can help you understand more about how He wants to help you see—how He wants to turn on the light for you! See you in Layer Three!

LAYER THREE: He Is the Way

Let's just take it slow and easy today and dig a little at a time! We have a little extra digging to do today. We will dig in John 10, and you will uncover two names!

1. See if you can unearth another name Jesus calls Himself and record it below.

⁷So Jesus said to them again, "Truly, truly, I say to you, I am the door of the sheep. ⁸"All who came

SPECIAL FIND!

At night flocks of sheep were kept in pens made of stone or branches with thorns. As the sheep went into the pen, the shepherd counted them to see if any were missing. The shepherd then slept in the only gap into the pen—the door to the pen. If wild animals came near, the shepherd was there to protect the sheep.

The shepherd was like the door to the sheep pen.

135

before Me are thieves and robbers, but the sheep did not hear them. ⁹"I am the door; if anyone enters through Me, he will be saved, and will go in and out and find pasture. ¹⁰"The thief comes only to steal and kill and destroy; I came that they may have life, and have *it* abundantly."

• Did you see that Jesus says, "I am the door of the sheep"? What else does He say in verse 9 about being a door?

What do you think of when you think of a door? Me too! I think of the way in and out!

Jesus is talking about being the door because He wants people to see that He is the *only* way to be saved. He says He is the only way in!

Lots of people think there are other ways to become a Christian and go to heaven. But when you hear people talk about other ways to heaven, remember that Jesus said He was the only door to salvation!

Aren't you glad that you know the way in? Aren't you happy that you are not confused about who can show you the way to be saved? Yes, Jesus is the door. And if you ask Him to show you how to come in, He will!

2. In this same chapter, Jesus calls Himself another name. Look for it in verses 11-15 and record it below these verses.

¹¹"I am the good shepherd; the good shepherd lays down His life for the sheep. ¹²"He who is a hired hand, and not a shepherd, who is not the owner of the sheep, sees the wolf coming, and leaves the sheep and flees, and the wolf snatches them and scatters *them*. ¹³"*He flees because he is a hired hand and is not concerned about the sheep.* ¹⁴"I am the good shepherd, and I know My own and My own know Me, ¹⁵even as the Father knows Me and I know the Father; and I lay down My life for the sheep."

• Did you see this name? Right! Now He calls Himself "the good shepherd." Let's see if we can find what He says about being a good shepherd. First look in verse 11 and write down what a good shepherd does for his sheep.

• Now read verse 14 again and see what He says about His sheep. Write it below.

What's in a Name?

• He repeats something in verse 15. When Jesus repeats something, it is very important. Write what He says He will do for His sheep.

Aren't you happy that Jesus is going to protect you? Aren't you amazed that He says He will die for you? Did He?

Remember that I said we were going to look at what Jesus did so you would believe? Well, it is still coming, but it has to do with dying for you! Can you see why He called Himself "the good shepherd"? Dying for you so you would not have to die is like the ultimate good anyone could ever do for you! Think about it for a moment.

So in this layer, we unearthed that Jesus is the door and the only way to salvation. And we discovered that He is the good shepherd who was willing to die for you—His sheep! Awesome! Thank Him that He cares so much about you!

LAYER FOUR: He Is Victory Over Death

Well, in this layer you have a bit of a head start. Aren't you glad? I know you are digging hard, and I am proud of you.

Let me tell you why you're ahead. You dug through a story about Jesus' friend Lazarus in Dig Eight. You will remember that Lazarus died and that Jesus raised him from the dead.

Well, after Jesus raised Lazarus, He called Himself the name we are going to uncover today. So you already know what was happening when Jesus calls Himself by this name.

1. Read John 11:25-26.

²⁵Jesus said to her, "I am the resurrection and the life; he who believes in Me will live even if he dies, ²⁶and everyone who lives and believes in Me will never die. Do you believe this?"

• What does He call Himself?

• Do you know that resurrection means to rise from the dead? Makes sense, doesn't it? Why would He use this name for Himself at this moment?

Right! He had just raised Lazarus from the dead and given him life again! Jesus knows that no one will forget this miracle, and He wants them to remember that *He* can give life! Aren't you glad that Jesus can give you spiritual life? Because He can, even after you die physically you will live again in heaven with Him. Tell Him what you think about the fact that He has power to give eternal life. Write what you think below.

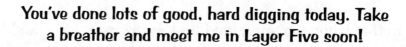

You've done lots of good, hard digging today. Take a breather and meet me in Layer Five soon!

LAYER FIVE: Is Jesus God's Son?

Today you will reach the bottom of Dig Nine. You have done an amazing job if you make it. It has been a hard but rewarding dig, hasn't it?

The name you will unearth today is one we have already uncovered before in Dig Two. But today you will discover lots more about this name, and you will need this important treasure when you start in Dig Ten. In that dig this name will help you understand why Jesus is arrested.

So don't stop digging until you hit bottom!

1. Read John 8:58-59 below.

⁵⁸Jesus said to them, "Truly, truly, I say to you, before Abraham was born, I am." ⁵⁹Therefore they picked up stones to throw at Him, but Jesus hid Himself and went out of the temple.

Can you think back to Dig Two where we talked about Jesus being one of God's three forms? Do you remember that we looked in Exodus 3:14 to see where God the Father called Himself "I AM"?

We talked then about the fact that Jesus also called Himself by that name. And we discovered that when He did, He was letting people know that He too was God.

Well, we have come back to that verse because it is one of the names Jesus calls Himself in the Gospel of John. And it is one of the names that shows us very clearly that Jesus claimed to be God's Son and a form of God.

Write John 8:58 below so you will remember it always.

What's in a Name?

• Read verse 59 again and see what happened when Jesus claimed to be God. What did the Jews do? (In this verse, the Jews are called "they.")

Do you know what stoning was? Well, it was a terrible way that people were put to death. A group of people would throw stones at one person until that person died!

Claiming to be equal to God was one reason a person could be stoned. And on this day, this is the reason the Jews were going to stone Jesus.

You see, don't you, that the Jews are not just having trouble thinking about who Jesus is now? They have gone beyond that point. Now, they are ready to kill Him!

• What does verse 59 say Jesus did?

So the Jews did not stone Jesus. But they wanted to. They did not believe He was God. And they thought it was a crime that He claimed to be God's Son—or to be God!

We will see in the next dig that the Jews did not give up on killing Jesus. They simply could not believe that He was who He said He was. And they felt it was their responsibility to do something to try and stop Him from claiming to be God!

2. I hope you will remember the names we have uncovered for Jesus—the names He called Himself.

                Bread of life   Good shepherd
                Light of the world   Resurrection and life
                Door   I AM

Take a few minutes and write what you think each name means. Also draw a quick sketch to help you remember the name. Don't do great art. Stick figures and rough sketches will be fine. Just a reminder! I will list the name, and you make the note and do the sketch!

Bread of life: Good shepherd:

Light of the world: Resurrection and life:

Door: I AM:

3. Think again about these names. Can you see how Jesus telling people His names could help Him reach His goal? Remember His goal was to help people believe so that He could save them! But they had to believe who He was to be saved.

These names were telling people about who He was and what He could do. Jesus knew some people would believe when they realized who He was. And some did!

I hope you will think about these names and what they mean between now and the next dig. You know He is all of these things for you!

4. Before you reach the very bottom of this amazing dig, you should try the puzzle on page 141. And then you will have hit the bottom and you can call it quits!

You have done an awesome job. I surely hope that you never, ever forget these names of Jesus and what they mean. You now have an incredible treasure to hold and study—six of His names! And because you know what they mean, you will see what they will mean to you! Dig Ten is coming up, and it is full of treasure. So rest up!

Truth Treasures for the Week

1.

2.

3.

Bury the Treasure:

For this is the will of My Father, that everyone who beholds the Son and believes in Him, may have eternal life; and I Myself will raise him up on the last day (John 6:40).

What's in a Name?

Name Hunt

In the following word hunt, find the 6 names of Jesus that we have been studying. I've also hidden 4 more names that you can do for fun. These 10 names of Jesus make us want to tell everyone how wonderful He is. Good luck on your hunt!

solution on page 197

Dig 10

The Beginning of the End

Tools of the Trade

1. Colored pencils
2. Pen or pencil
3. Dictionary
4. Jesus' Last Hours on pages 156-157
5. An Alphanumber of Promise on page 158

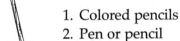

Directions for Diggers

We have come to a dig that will be very special for you because you will discover what Jesus said to the men He loved so much just before He prepared to die. And you will see something that He asked His Father to do *for you*! Yes, for you! Hard to believe or what! Jesus prayed for you, and you will uncover that prayer in this dig!

Let's get a move on. That means: Let's get going because it is too good to wait! But don't forget to check in with headquarters as you get moving—that is part of moving!

LAYER ONE: The Pressure Builds Up

The Jews were becoming very nervous because Jesus was so powerful and because so many people were believing in Him. Let's remember what we have discovered about how they were feeling and what they wanted to do—just as a review.

Truth Trackers: *Jesus Our Savior and Friend*

1. We discovered in Dig Seven that some of the Jews were bothered by the fact that when Jesus healed the lame man He had the man pick up his mat and walk. You will remember that they were upset because it was the Sabbath and they did not think that work should be done on that day. And not only did they think that Jesus did work by healing the man, they also thought that He had the man do work by walking with his mat! Read the verses below as a reminder.

14Now it was a Sabbath on the day when Jesus made the clay and opened his eyes. **15**Then the Pharisees also were asking him again how he received his sight. And he said to them, "He applied clay to my eyes, and I washed, and I see." **16**Therefore some of the Pharisees were saying, "This man is not from God, because He does not keep the Sabbath." But others were saying, "How can a man who is a sinner perform such signs?" And there was a division among them. (John 9:14-16)

2. Then in the last dig, we uncovered that the Jews were becoming more and more upset. They were really angry because Jesus said that He was from heaven! They talked about Him being Joseph's son. They could not believe that He would claim to be God's Son—or to be equal with God. This claim went too far in their minds. We saw that some of them even tried to stone Him to death. Read these verses so you can see what they said again.

41Therefore the Jews were grumbling about Him, because He said, "I am the bread that came down out of heaven." **42**They were saying, "Is not this Jesus, the son of Joseph, whose father and mother we know? How does He now say, 'I have come down out of heaven'?" (John 6:41-42)

13So the Pharisees said to Him, "You are testifying about Yourself; Your testimony is not true." **14**Jesus answered and said to them, "Even if I testify about Myself, My testimony is true, for I know where I came from and where I am going; but you do not know where I come from or where I am going. (John 8:13-14)

3. So we know that the Jews are reaching a point where they feel like they need to do away with Jesus. Do you remember in Dig Eight when Jesus raised Lazarus from the dead that the Pharisees got a group together to talk about what to do? They said if something wasn't done to stop Jesus that *all* men would believe! Read the verses following again to help refresh your memory.

The Beginning of the End

⁴⁷Therefore the chief priests and the Pharisees convened a council, and were saying, "What are we doing? For this man is performing many signs. ⁴⁸If we let Him *go on* like this, all men will believe in Him, and the Romans will come and take away both our place and our nation." (John 11:47-48)

4. In Dig Nine, you unearthed one of the names Jesus called Himself: I AM. I mentioned to you then that this was the name that got Him in lots of trouble because it is the name He used that made these men see that He was claiming to be God. Let's see why they thought that.

⁵⁸Jesus said to them, "Truly, truly, I say to you, before Abraham was born, I am." ⁵⁹Therefore they picked up stones to throw at Him, but Jesus hid Himself and went out of the temple. (John 8:58-59)

- Who does Jesus say He existed before?

Right. He says He was around *before* Abraham. Well, when Jesus was living, it had been about 4,000 years since Abraham had been alive on earth! So they realized that if Jesus was saying that He was *before* Abraham that He was claiming to have been around even further back than 4,000 years! And if He had been around that long, He was claiming that He was God!

5. Then in the next verse we saw that they wanted to stone Jesus. The Pharisees were determined to stop Jesus. They knew that He was powerful because they had seen the miracles. And they knew that people were believing in Him. They were afraid of what may happen if He was not stopped. In their minds, it was time for Him to die!

It is sad, isn't it? To think that men wanted to kill the Son of God. But don't forget why He came! He came to save sinners, and dying was a part of the plan. Don't forget either, that we are going to discover what He did for you so that you would believe. And that dying was a part of that too! Think about these things, and meet me soon in Layer Two.

LAYER TWO: Not Until God Was Ready!

In Layer One, we discovered that the Pharisees were getting very uneasy. They were so nervous that they were ready to get rid of Jesus! That is pretty nervous, isn't it? But you will remember too that when they tried to get near Him to stone Him, He got away.

Let's dig through some verses that will help us understand how He got away when they wanted to stone Him. These verses will help us see too why He did not escape when they decided to crucify Him.

Truth Trackers: *Jesus Our Savior and Friend*

1. You discovered in John 8:59 that the Jews tried to stone Jesus. But they had tried several other times to arrest Him. Let's dig through verses about some of these times and see why they seemed to be unable to capture Him when they tried.

³⁰So they were seeking to seize Him; and no man laid his hand on Him, because His hour had not yet come. (John 7:30)

If you read more of this chapter, you would unearth the fact that Jesus had been talking about being sent to earth from heaven, from God. And you know how nervous the Pharisees would get when He talked like that.

But what do you see in verse 30 about why they could not capture Him when they tried to seize Him? Write it below.

2. Let's look at another time when Jesus was talking about being "the light of the world." Do you remember digging to find that name in Dig Nine? Well, after Jesus called Himself by this name and said God had sent Him to earth to be the light, let's see what happened.

²⁰These words He spoke in the treasury, as He taught in the temple; and no one seized Him, because His hour had not yet come. (John 8:20)

Why does this verse say that no one seized Him?

3. What do you think the Bible means when it says that "His hour had not come?" Try and write an explanation.

I agree with you. I think it means that none of these times when they tried to capture Jesus were the time that *God* had planned for Him to be taken and killed.

4. Now, let's see what Jesus says about the time that we are going to begin digging through in the next few layers.

¹Jesus spoke these things; and lifting up His eyes to heaven, He said, "Father, the hour has come; glorify Your Son, that the Son may glorify You…" (John 17:1)

The Beginning of the End

- What does Jesus say about His time?

- What does He ask His Father to do in this time?

- What does He say He will do?

So we have uncovered a very important fact: There was an hour—an exact moment in time—when Jesus was supposed to die. And He says in the verse you just dug through that the time has come.

So can you see why the Pharisees couldn't get to Him before? It wasn't the right time! It wasn't *God's* time!

Jesus also says that now since the time is right the Father will be glorified—and so will the Son.

In the next several layers, we are going to look at what Jesus says to the 12 men He had asked to work with Him—the 12 men who had become His closest friends. He spent some special time with them and talked with them about many things before He told them His time had come to die.

And in the next couple of digs, we will try to discover what He meant when He said He would glorify the Father. And we will look for what He meant when He said the Father would glorify Him.

You are finding some incredible, valuable treasures! Hang on to them all! And meet me soon in Layer Three!

LAYER THREE: Jesus Washes Their Feet

Jesus loved the 12 men very much that He had asked to work with Him. And now that He knew it was time for Him to die, He went away with them from all of the crowds of people who were always around Him. He wanted to have a last dinner with them alone.

1. In the next two layers, let's dig through some things He did with them and things He told them while He was alone with them. But first let's see what I just told you about in the Bible verses themselves.

¹Now before the Feast of the Passover, Jesus knowing that His hour had come that He would depart out of this world to the Father, having loved His own who were in

the world, He loved them to the end. **2**During supper, the devil having already put into the heart of Judas Iscariot, *the son* of Simon, to betray Him, **3***Jesus*, knowing that the Father had given all things into His hands, and that He had come forth from God and was going back to God, **4**got up from supper, and laid aside His garments; and taking a towel, He girded Himself. **5**Then He poured water into the basin, and began to wash the disciples' feet and to wipe them with the towel with which He was girded. (John 13:1-5)

• What does verse 1 say Jesus knew?

Yes, again we see that He knew His hour had come—the time for Him to die was now!

• In verse 1 the 12 men are called "His own." How does it say He felt about them?

• You see something very sad about one of the men—about Judas. What do you uncover about him?

Verse 3 tells us what we have already uncovered: That Jesus knew He had come from God and was going back to God. Remember Jesus talking about this very thing had upset the Pharisees so much they wanted Jesus dead!

• In verses 4-5, what do you see Jesus do for the disciples?

The Beginning of the End

In Israel, where these men lived, only a servant washed another man's feet. Jesus was showing them that He loved them and wanted to be a servant to them. They did not understand how He would *really* serve them, but they were going to see very soon!

So we see that Jesus was spending a last evening with these men He loved. As He washes their feet, He talks with them. Then He eats a meal with them and talks about lots of other things. In the next layer, we are going to see some of the very important things He says to them. And we will uncover something too that He says to God about you!

You are gathering very, very rare treasures. Hold them up and look carefully at them because not many people ever get to see these the way you will! I look forward to Layer Four since we will discover some very private and important things Jesus said to the men He loved.

LAYER FOUR: Special Instructions for His Followers

In the next two layers, you will discover some amazing treasure! The things Jesus said to these men He loved are very special, and you will unearth some of the *most* special of these special things.

1. Before you begin to see what Jesus talks with these men about, look at one important section of Scripture. This section will help you discover what happened to Judas.

²⁶Jesus then answered˙, "That is the one for whom I shall dip the morsel and give it to him." So when He had dipped the morsel, He took˙ and gave˙ it to Judas, *the son* of Simon Iscariot. ²⁷After the morsel, Satan then entered into him. Therefore Jesus said˙ to him, "What you do, do quickly." ²⁸Now no one of those reclining *at the table* knew for what purpose He had said this to him. ²⁹For some were supposing, because Judas had the money box, that Jesus was saying to him, "Buy the things we have need of for the feast"; or else, that he should give something to the poor. ³⁰So after receiving the morsel he went out immediately; and it was night. (John 13:26-30)

Truth Trackers: Jesus Our Savior and Friend

Remember that you have discovered that Jesus was omniscient—that He knew everything. Well, because this is true, He knew that Judas would betray him.

- Do you know what *betray* means? Look it up and write what it means.

It is terrible to think that one of the men who had been so close to Jesus would now tell the Pharisees where to find Him and arrest Him, isn't it? But you can see by what you just read that it was a part of the big plan.

- Do the other men know what is happening? Look at verse 28.

2. Now what I wanted you to discover is that when Jesus began talking to the men and telling them special things, Judas—the one who was going to betray Him—was gone!
So let's begin to see what Jesus said to the 11 men who are left with Him.

33"Little children, I am with you a little while longer. You will seek Me; and as I said to the Jews, now I also say to you, 'Where I am going, you cannot come.' **34**"A new commandment I give to you, that you love one another, even as I have loved you, that you also love one another. **35**"By this all men will know that you are My disciples, if you have love for one another." **36**Simon Peter said˙ to Him, "Lord, where are You going?" Jesus answered, "Where I go, you cannot follow Me now; but you will follow later." (John 13:33-36)

- Jesus loves these men so much He calls them a special name: little children. In verse 33, what does He tell them they will not be able to do?

- In verse 34, what is the commandment He gives to them now that He is leaving?

- In verse 35, He tells them why He wants them to love each other. Why?

The Beginning of the End

• In verse 36, Jesus tells them when they will be able to come to the place He is going. When?

3. Now let's see another amazing thing He tells these men.

¹"Do not let your heart be troubled; believe in God, believe also in Me. ²"In My Father's house are many dwelling places; if it were not so, I would have told you; for I go to prepare a place for you. ³"If I go and prepare a place for you, I will come again and receive you to Myself, that where I am, *there* you may be also.
¹⁵"If you love Me, you will keep My commandments." (John 14:1-3,15)

• Jesus tells them not to be troubled—not to worry. He goes on and tells them to believe in God and in Him. What does He say next about His Father's house?

• In verse 2, what does He tell them He is going to do for them?

• Then in verse 3, what does He say He will do?

• Where does He promise these men they will be? Look at the end of verse 3?

• In verse 15, He gives them another instruction. He tells them if they love Him that they will do it. What is it?

Wow! Jesus is saying some pretty awesome things: That He is going away and that they can't come until later. And that He is going to prepare a place for them to come. And then He will take them to be with Him!
And He is asking them to do some amazing things: Love one another like He has loved them! And to keep His commandments!
Think about what Jesus promised and about what He asked. And think about the fact that He loves you as much as He loved these men. And think about the fact that He wants

you to be with Him one day! But in the meantime, realize that He wants you to love others and obey Him—these things will help other people want to know about Him.

How incredible to think you can be with Jesus one day! And how incredible to think that while you are on earth you can live in a way that will make others want to know Him and be with Him too!

4. Turn to pages 156-157 and look at the drawing Jesus' Last Hours. You will see a sketch of the city of Jerusalem—the city where Jesus will die. In squares around the sketch of the city you will find events that were a part of His last hours. Look at the drawings in the squares and color the event you are unearthing at this point—the last supper that Jesus eats with His men.

Lots to think about—and lots of decisions to make! Ask your parents to talk with you about what you have uncovered today. It is all very important stuff! And meet me in Layer Five as soon as you can!

LAYER FIVE: Promises for You and Me

Let's dig today to see some of the other marvelous things Jesus shared with the 11 men who were closest to Him while He was on the earth.

1. Read the verses below to see what Jesus tells these men about prayer. I think you will be surprised by what He said!

7"If you abide in Me, and My words abide in you, ask whatever you wish, and it will be done for you." (John 15:7)

First, do you know what the word *abide* means? It means *to live in*. The way Jesus uses it in talking to these men, it means "to live in, to be at home in." Think about that and read the verse again.

• What does He say to them about what they can ask of Him?

• Does He say that He will do it?

• What does He say has to happen for them to be able to ask so that He will do whatever they ask? There are two things. I'll help you a little.

If you _____ __ _____ AND __ _____ _____ in you

The Beginning of the End

Do you see that Jesus is saying that these men need to live in Him—do what He asks them to do AND that they need to let His words or the things that He has taught them live in them?

If a person lives their life in the Lord Jesus Christ, they want to do what He wants. And if they know the Bible, His Word, and let it live in them they know what He wants them to do.

You may wonder how He can make this wonderful promise! But remember if you live in Him and His word lives in you then this is a possibility. If these things are true, you will pray in a way that means He can answer because you will want things that are like God!

2. Next we will dig into two verses that show what Jesus promised about the Holy Spirit. Do you remember that there are three forms to God? The Holy Spirit is the one we have talked about only a little, but now you will see that Jesus talks about Him.

7"But I tell you the truth, it is to your advantage that I go away; for if I do not go away, the Helper will not come to you; but if I go, I will send Him to you."

13"But when He, the Spirit of truth, comes, He will guide you into all the truth; for He will not speak on His own initiative, but whatever He hears, He will speak; and He will disclose to you what is to come." (John 16:7,13)

Jesus calls the Holy Spirit "the Helper" in verse 7. He says that He must go away for the Helper to come.

• In verse 13, Jesus calls the Holy Spirit "the Spirit of truth." What does He say that He will do when He comes?

I know you remember that we talked about the Holy Spirit helping you understand truth as you dig through the Bible, and now you see Jesus talking about that very thing!

So Jesus is gone, and we can't see Him now on earth. But when He left, another person who is one of the forms of God came to earth—the Holy Spirit. The Holy Spirit is with us today! We can't see Him either because He is a Spirit. He does not have a body. But when you know God's Word and when you listen and want to know what to do, the Holy Spirit works in your heart so that you understand what to do.

FOR ME!!!

3. Now you are going to see something pretty awesome! Jesus prays to His Father for these men *and* for you! We don't have time to dig deep enough to see all that He prayed, but we will dig far enough to discover a couple of things. Can you believe He prayed for you?

17"Sanctify them in the truth; Your word is truth.

20"I do not ask on behalf of these alone, but for those also who believe in Me through their word…"

24"Father, I desire that they also, whom You have given Me, be with Me where I am, so that they may see My glory which You have given Me, for You loved Me before the foundation of the world." (John 17:17,20,24)

- Jesus asks God to do something in verse 17. What does He ask?

Yes, He asks that God sanctify them in truth. *Sanctify* means *to set apart*. Jesus asks God to set them apart through the truth of the Word of God. You are being set apart in that way as you have been digging out truth. You are set apart because you now know some things that other boys and girls don't—the truth you know sets you apart. You can be different if you obey what you know! This is part of what Jesus asks God to do.

Then in verse 20, you discover that Jesus is not asking just for the men He is with. He is also asking for those who will hear of Him and believe by what they tell others—by their word. You are one of these who heard from these men! You have been studying the books these men wrote. Jesus prayed for *you*! And He asked that you be set apart by truth!

So the reason you have been digging through truth and understanding it is that Jesus prayed for you! Awesome or what!

He prays that you will be with Him in verse 24. He wants all those He loves to see His glory—to be with Him and His Father. To live for eternity with them!

Can you believe it! Even as He was preparing to die, Jesus prayed for you!

We are almost to the end of Jesus' life on earth. But really the exciting part is just beginning! In our next dig, you will see how He goes to the cross for you. Remember that it is all a part of God's plan. And remember we will see what He does so that you will believe!

4. Find the Timeline of Christ on pages 191-192 and chart the event you uncovered in this dig.

The Beginning of the End

Take a good break. Rest. Think. Thank God for all He did so that you could be saved! And I will see you later in Dig Eleven!

Don't forget your work below and your puzzle.

TRUTH TREASURES FOR THE WEEK

1.

2.

3.

BURY THE TREASURE:

He who has my commandments and keeps them, he it is who loves Me (John 14:21a).

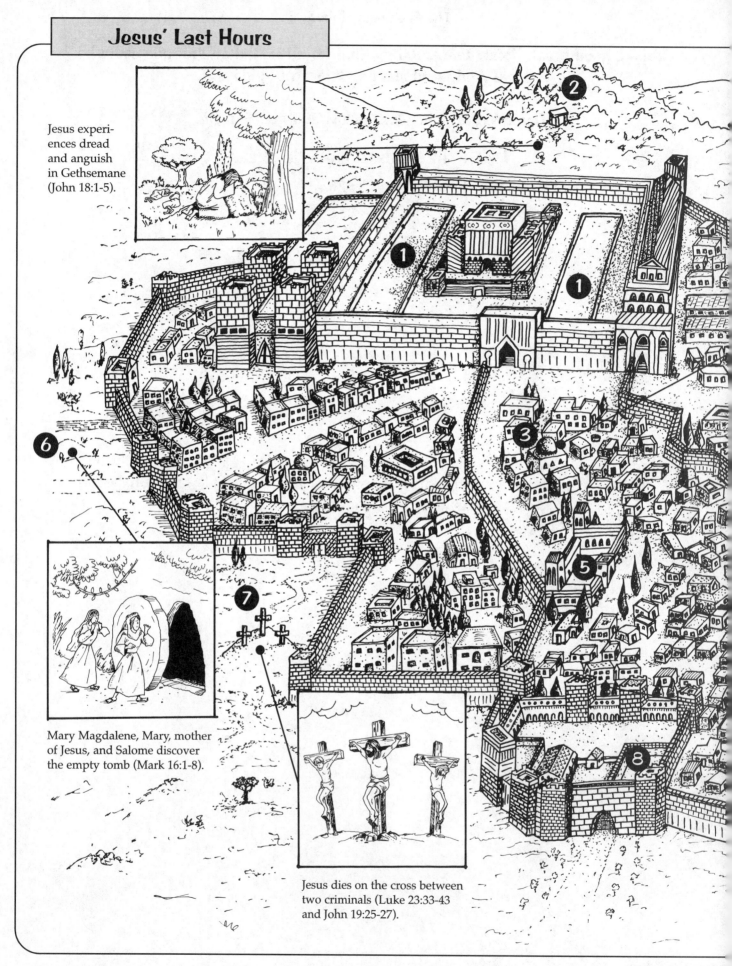

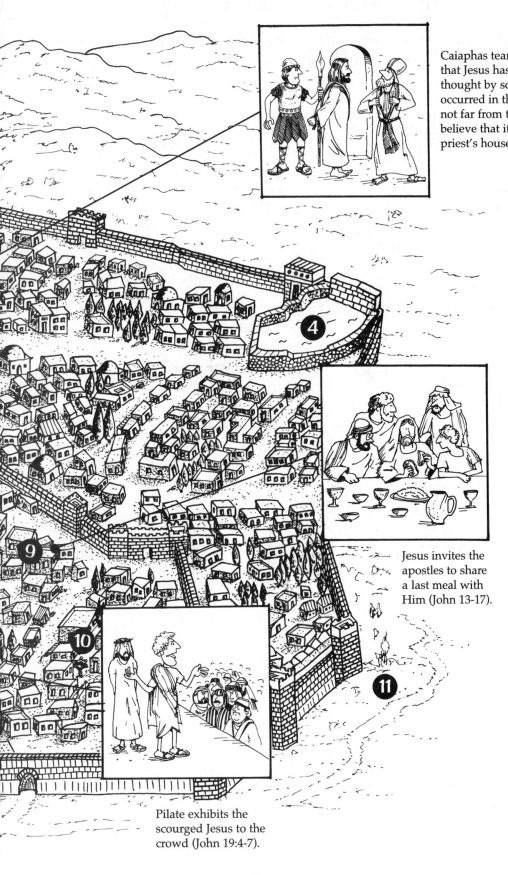

Caiaphas tears his robes, declaring that Jesus has blasphemed. It is thought by some that this scene occurred in the Sanhedrin building not far from the temple. Others believe that it occurred in the high priest's house (Matthew 26:62-66).

Jesus invites the apostles to share a last meal with Him (John 13-17).

Pilate exhibits the scourged Jesus to the crowd (John 19:4-7).

1. Forecourt of the Gentiles
2. Mount of Olives
3. Hall of the Sanhedrin
4. Pool of Siloam (John 9:7)
5. Palace of Herod Antipas (Luke 23:6-12)
6. Location of Joseph of Aramethea's tomb
7. Golgotha
8. Palace of Governor Pontius Pilate
9. House of Caiaphas
10. Room of last supper (cenacle)
11. Valley of Gehenna

Truth Trackers

An Alphanumber Promise

There are numbers in each square of the diagram below. The numbers represent letters of the alphabet. Change the numbers to letters and discover one of the great promises of Jesus.

A 1	B 2	C 3	D 4	E 5	F 6	G 7	H 8	I 9	J 10	K 11	L 12	M 13	N 14
O 15	P 16	Q 17	R 18	S 19	T 20	U 21	V 22	W 23	X 24	Y 25	Z 26	Space 27

9	27	23	9	12	12	27	3	15	13	5
27	1	7	1	9	14	27	1	14	4	27
18	5	3	5	9	22	5	27	25	15	21
27	20	15	27	13	25	19	5	12	6	27
20	8	1	20	27	23	8	5	18	5	27
9	27	1	13	27	20	8	5	18	5	27
25	15	21	27	13	1	25	27	2	5	27
1	12	19	15	27	10	15	8	14		14:3b

solution on page 198

Dig 11

The Famous Trial of Jesus

Tools of the Trade

1. Colored pencils
2. Pen or pencil
3. Dictionary
4. Jesus' Last Hours on pages 156-157
5. A Time to Pray on page 170

Directions for Diggers

We are coming now to the two digs that are probably going to be your biggest challenge. Dig Eleven is the first of the two. But I think it may be a challenge for a different reason than some of the others have been.

This dig will unearth some treasures that do not look as awesome at first glance because they are truths about some of the things that happened to Jesus in His last hours before He went to the cross.

BUT in the end, when we finish with this dig and the one that follows, I think you will find that these digs have helped you uncover the most awesome treasures of all. Often, the most valuable treasures are the ones that are the most difficult to discover. The treasures you will uncover in these digs are the ones that show Jesus reached His goal! They show that He made it to the end. And they show that He was the victor!

Let's begin to look at these last hard, difficult hours of Jesus' life and remember that in the end, He wins the battle!

Truth Trackers: Jesus Our Savior and Friend

Don't forget to check in with headquarters. You will need help in understanding what we will uncover!

LAYER ONE: Jesus Is Arrested

Let's get started right away. This is a great dig, and I don't want to use your digging time by talking too much!

1. Read the verses below and think about where we stopped digging in Dig Ten. Jesus was telling the men He loved some special things, and He had just prayed for them.

¹When Jesus had spoken these words, He went forth with His disciples over the ravine of the Kidron, where there was a garden, in which He entered with His disciples. (John 18:1)

When Jesus finished talking with His men and praying for them, where do they go?

2. Let's look in another gospel to see the name of the garden and some of what happened there.

³⁶Then Jesus came* with them to a place called Gethsemane, and said* to His disciples, "Sit here while I go over there and pray." (Matthew 26:36)

• What was the name of the garden? I bet you have heard people talk about it before because it is so famous!

• Why did Jesus go there?

3. Now dig through Matthew 26:39 and see what He prayed about.

³⁹And He went a little beyond *them*, and fell on His face and prayed, saying, "My Father, if it is possible, let this cup pass from Me; yet not as I will, but as You will."

• What did He do before He began to pray. I'll help you find this treasure!

    And He _____ __ ___ _____ them

    and _____ __ ___ _____ _____ _____

Yes, He went far enough from His friends to be alone. Then, He fell on His face to talk to His Father. He knew what was coming, and He felt the pressure of all that would happen.

The Famous Trial of Jesus

• What does He say to His Father? Write what He prays.

Do you know that "the cup" He talks about is the fact that He is going to die on a cross? He is telling His Father that He wishes there was another way to save the world. But He says if there isn't that He will do it!

4. Now let's discover who shows up again.

²Now Judas also, who was betraying Him, knew the place, for Jesus had often met there with His disciples. ³Judas then, having received the *Roman* cohort and officers from the chief priests and the Pharisees, came˙ there with lanterns and torches and weapons. ⁴So Jesus, knowing all the things that were coming upon Him, went forth and said˙ to them, "Whom do you seek?" ⁵They answered Him, "Jesus the Nazarene." He said˙ to them, "I am *He*." And Judas also, who was betraying Him, was standing with them. (John 18:2-5)

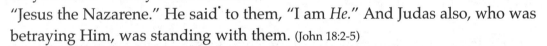

• Who comes with the men to arrest Jesus?

• Yes, Judas brings the soldiers to arrest Jesus. Does Jesus try to run? What does He say?

Jesus has now been arrested. The things that will lead to His death are now happening. In Layer Two, we will begin to dig through the verses that tell about His trial and about the sentence that He was given—death on a cross!

5. Turn to the Timeline of the Life of Christ on pages 191-192 and mark the two events you have uncovered.

6. Turn to the drawing of Jesus' Last Hours on pages 156-157 and color the sketch of Jesus praying in the Garden.

Rest up. I know this is hard to think about. But you need to keep thinking about the fact that in the end JESUS WINS!

Truth Trackers: Jesus Our Savior and Friend

LAYER TWO: The Trial Begins

In this layer, you will unearth treasures about the famous trial of Jesus. The trial is a bit of a puzzle to follow. One of the reasons it can be a puzzle to sort through is because there was no real reason to kill Jesus. But the religious leaders wanted to do away with Him, so they had to find a legitimate reason that He could be put to death. It was not an easy task! Trying to find a reason meant that one man kept sending Jesus to another man hoping that maybe he would come up with a good reason.

You know that Jesus lived in Israel and was Jewish. But what we have not talked about is that when He lived on earth the Romans were ruling in Israel. They had captured the country, and they were ruling the government. First, you will see that the Jewish leaders questioned Jesus, and then you will see them send Him to the Roman ruler—all in an attempt to find a reason to put Him to death.

Ready. Let's dig slowly and carefully, thinking as we work.

1. Let's go back now to the garden in our minds and remember that Jesus has just been arrested by Roman soldiers. Where do they take Jesus when they arrest Him?

12So the *Roman* cohort and the commander and the officers of the Jews, arrested Jesus and bound Him, **13**and led Him to Annas first; for he was father-in-law of Caiaphas, who was high priest that year. (John 18:12-13)

2. Yes, they take Jesus to the father-in-law of the High Priest. His name is Annas.

19The high priest then questioned Jesus about His disciples, and about His teaching. **20**Jesus answered him, "I have spoken openly to the world; I always taught in synagogues and in the temple, where all the Jews come together; and I spoke nothing in secret. **21**"Why do you question Me? Question those who have heard what I spoke to them; they know what I said." **22**When He had said this, one of the officers standing nearby struck Jesus, saying, "Is that the way You answer the high priest?" **23**Jesus answered him, "If I have spoken wrongly, testify of the wrong; but if rightly, why do you strike Me?" **24**So Annas sent Him bound to Caiaphas the high priest. (John 18:19-24)

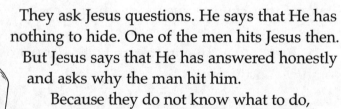

They ask Jesus questions. He says that He has nothing to hide. One of the men hits Jesus then. But Jesus says that He has answered honestly and asks why the man hit him.

Because they do not know what to do, they send Jesus on now to the High Priest. This man was the head of the Jewish religious leaders. His name is Caiaphias. So they begin at the top of the Jewish system to see if they can find a reason to kill Jesus.

The Famous Trial of Jesus

3. Let's find what the High Priest and his men ask Jesus. And let's find how He answers.

⁵⁴Peter had followed Him at a distance, right into the courtyard of the high priest; and he was sitting with the officers and warming himself at the fire. ⁵⁵Now the chief priests and the whole Council kept trying to obtain testimony against Jesus to put Him to death, and they were not finding any. ⁵⁶For many were giving false testimony against Him, but their testimony was not consistent. (Mark 14:54-56)

• What do you discover about the information they were trying to get from Jesus so that they could put Him to death? Dig in verse 55.

• In verse 56, you uncover that people were willing to even lie to try and trap Jesus. But what happens when these people start to lie?

4. Find the drawing on pages 156-157, Jesus' Last Hours, and color the sketch of Jesus before Caiaphas.

These men worked all night to try and figure out a reason to kill Jesus, but they couldn't! When morning came, they tried another idea. Let's take a break and then begin digging here in Layer Three to see if we can find what happened next.

This is hard digging because we are working through verses that have such sad things happening. But the good news is coming!

LAYER THREE: No Reason Can Be Found

When we stopped digging in Layer Two, the Jewish leaders had come to a point that they didn't know what to do with Jesus. They wanted to kill Him, but they can't find a legal reason to kill him.

So now they are going to the highest court in the land—to the Romans. And you will meet the ruler of the Roman government in Jerusalem, a man named Pilate. You will briefly encounter another Roman who ruled in a different area of the country called Galillee—a man called Herod.

1. This is a long section of Scripture, but it is important to dig through because you will see that Pilate couldn't find a reason to kill Jesus either. Read this section, and then we will talk about some of what you discover.

²⁸They led Jesus therefore from Caiaphas into the Praetorium, and it was early; and they themselves did not enter into the Praetorium in order that they might not be

defiled, but might eat the Passover. ²⁹Pilate therefore went out to them, and said, "What accusation do you bring against this Man?" ³⁰They answered and said to him, "If this Man were not an evildoer, we would not have delivered Him up to you." ³¹Pilate therefore said to them, "Take Him yourselves, and judge Him according to your law." The Jews said to him, "We are not permitted to put anyone to death." ³²that the word of Jesus might be fulfilled, which He spoke, signifying by what kind of death He was about to die.
³³Pilate therefore entered again into the Praetorium, and summoned Jesus, and said to Him, "Are You the King of the Jews?" ³⁴Jesus answered, "Are you saying this on your own initiative, or did others tell you about Me?" ³⁵Pilate answered, "I am not a Jew, am I? Your own nation and the chief priests delivered You up to me; what have You done?" ³⁶Jesus answered, "My kingdom is not of this world. If My kingdom were of this world, then My servants would be fighting, that I might not be delivered up to the Jews; but as it is, My kingdom is not of this realm." ³⁷Pilate therefore said to Him, "So You are a king?" Jesus answered, "You say *correctly* that I am a king. For this I have been born, and for this I have come into the world, to bear witness to the truth. Everyone who is of the truth hears my voice." ³⁸Pilate said to Him, "What is truth?" And when he had said this, he went out again to the Jews and said to them, "I find no guilt in Him." (John 18:28-38)

• Read verse 31 again and think about what the Jews say. Write it below.

Now we learn that they are not able to sentence Jesus to death! No wonder they have gone to the Romans for help!

• Pilate asks if Jesus is a King, and He says that He is. But He goes on to say that He isn't a King in this world. He is a King of heaven! And Jesus says something in verse 37 that you will recognize—about a witness. Write it below.

Remember when we discovered in Dig Nine that the Pharisees said Jesus' witness was not true? But we learned it was, and now here again He gives witness that He has come to earth to tell people the truth...so that they can believe and hear His voice!

• Look again in verse 38 and uncover what Pilate says to the Jews about Jesus.

The Famous Trial of Jesus

2. Now something surprising happened.

⁴Then Pilate said to the chief priests and the crowds, "I find no guilt in this man." ⁵But they kept on insisting, saying, "He stirs up the people, teaching all over Judea, starting from Galilee even as far as this place." ⁶But when Pilate heard it, he asked whether the man was a Galilean. ⁷And when he learned that He belonged to Herod's jurisdiction, he sent Him to Herod, who himself also was in Jerusalem at that time. (Luke 23:4-7)

Pilate doesn't want to convict an innocent man either. So he finds out that Jesus really lives in the Galilee area and decides to have the man who governs the area Jesus lives in talk to Jesus. This man's name is Herod, and he just happened to be visiting in Jerusalem!

To better understand why Pilate could ask Herod to question Jesus, think of this: It would be like the governor of California finding out that a man he is talking to about a crime was from the state of New York. And then he knew too that the governor of New York was in town! He would ask the governor of New York to talk to the man. Let's look at what happened next.

3. Let's discover what happened when Herod gets into the picture.

⁸Now Herod was very glad when he saw Jesus; for he had wanted to see Him for a long time, because he had been hearing about Him and was hoping to see some sign performed by Him. ⁹And he questioned Him at some length; but He answered him nothing. ¹⁰And the chief priests and the scribes were standing there, accusing Him vehemently. ¹¹And Herod with his soldiers, after treating Him with contempt and mocking Him, dressed Him in a gorgeous robe and sent Him back to Pilate. ¹²Now Herod and Pilate became friends with one another that very day; for before they had been enemies with each other. ¹³Pilate summoned the chief priests and the rulers and the people, ¹⁴and said to them, "You brought this man to me as one who incites the people to rebellion, and behold, having examined Him before you, I have found no guilt in this man regarding the charges which you make against Him. ¹⁵"No, nor has Herod, for he sent Him back to us; and behold, nothing deserving death has been done by Him." (Luke 23:8-15)

- How did Herod feel about the fact that he was going to meet Jesus?

Read verse 11 again. You discover that Herod and his soldiers were very mean to Jesus. They even put a robe on Him to make fun of the fact that He said He was a King.

- What does this verse say they did in the end? Who do they send Jesus to talk to after they finish with Him?

Truth Trackers: Jesus Our Savior and Friend

• What happened on that day for Pilate and Herod according to verse 12?

• Read verse 14 again slowly. What does Pilate say that Herod found Jesus guilty of?

• In verse 15, what does he say Herod found Jesus guilty of?

Yes, neither man could find any reason to kill Jesus. You will not believe what happened next! Just think about what you uncovered in Dig Ten when Jesus said that His hour had come. Even though no one can find a legal reason to kill Him, it is time for Him to die—*God's* time!

I will be in Layer Four and will be ready to go when you are. But I know you need a rest and time to think about all you are uncovering. Just keep on thinking about Jesus winning in the end. Because He does!

LAYER FOUR: Pilate Passes Jesus to Herod

Pilate does not want to convict Jesus. He can't find a reason to. But let's see what happened that made him send Jesus to the cross. Don't forget that "His hour had come!"

1. You will find Luke 23:15 in this section again so you will begin digging where we stopped yesterday. Then, you will see in the rest of the section what happened that made Pilate send Jesus to His death.

¹⁵"No, nor has Herod, for he sent Him back to us; and behold, nothing deserving death has been done by Him. ¹⁶"Therefore I will punish Him and release Him." ¹⁷*Now he was obliged to release to them at the feast one prisoner.* ¹⁸But they cried out all together, saying, "Away with this man, and release for us Barabbas!" ¹⁹(He was one who had been thrown into prison for an insurrection made in the city, and for murder.) ²⁰Pilate, wanting to release Jesus, addressed them again, ²¹but they kept on calling out, saying, "Crucify, crucify Him!" ²²And he said to them the third time, "Why, what evil has this man done? I have found in Him no guilt *demanding* death; therefore I will punish Him and release Him." ²³But they were insistent, with loud voices asking that He be crucified. And their voices *began* to prevail. ²⁴And Pilate pronounced sentence that their demand be granted. ²⁵And he released the man they were asking for who had been thrown into prison for insurrection and murder, but he delivered Jesus to their will.

The Famous Trial of Jesus

Jesus was in town for Passover, one of the celebrations of the Jews. You will remember in an earlier dig finding out that when Jesus was 12 years old, He went to this celebration and that Jewish men went each year. In verse 17, you discover that at this celebration it was a rule that a prisoner was set free. Pilate hoped that he could use this rule to set Jesus free!

• But dig in verse 18 and see what the crowd yelled.

• Verse 20 gives us a great treasure. What do you find about Pilate?

Yes, he tried again to get the people to agree to free Jesus!

• What do you find in verse 21 about how the crowd responded to Pilate's plea?

• You won't believe what Pilate does in verse 22. Hurry and find it.

Yes, a third time he asks them to agree to free Jesus. Pilate knew He was not guilty!

• Dig through verses 23-25 again to see what happened in the end. What happened?

We see that in the end, Jesus is condemned to die on a cross. Not because He is guilty. But because His hour has come and because He came to save people. Remember hours earlier He had asked His Father if there was another way. This was a horrible way to die. But this death was a part of His Father's plan—Jesus would go to the cross for *you* and all the people of the world!

2. Turn to the drawing Jesus' Last Hours on pages 156-157 and find the sketch that represents the event you dug out today. Color the sketch.

I will be ready to work through Layer Five when you are. Why don't you ask your mom or dad to work in it with you. It is a lot to dig through and understand. But as we keep saying—in the end...what happens? Yes, Jesus wins!

Truth Trackers: Jesus Our Savior and Friend

LAYER FIVE: The Real Reason for Jesus' Death

I know you understand that Jesus had to die because His hour had come, but I want to be sure you understand why God asked Him to die at this time. Let's see what we discover.

1. Go way back in your mind for a moment and think about what you discovered when we walked through the Garden of Eden. Not the Garden of Gethsemane. The Garden of Eden with Adam and Eve.

They sinned, didn't they? And when they sinned, all mankind became sinners. God had told them that if they sinned they would die—spiritually. So now man will die physically and spiritually. And God does not want us to die spiritually. He wants us to live spiritually while we are on earth and to live with Him and His Son in heaven after our bodies die.

But for us to live spiritually, there is a price to be paid.

²³For the wages of sin is death, but the free gift of God is eternal life in Christ Jesus our Lord. (Romans 6:23)

• What is the price for sin?

SIN = SPIRITUAL DEATH

Yes. Sin had a price, and it is death. To pay for our sin, someone had to die. And so that you would not have to die to pay that price, Jesus said He would. And God agreed.

• Dig in verse 23 again and write below what the gift is.

• Where is the gift found?

2. Now dig in Mark 10:45 and see what you find about why Jesus came to earth. Write two things you discover.

⁴⁵"For even the Son of Man did not come to be served, but to serve, and to give His life a ransom for many."

3. Write out the two reasons.

• to _____

• to give _____ _____ ___ _____ _____ _____

The Famous Trial of Jesus

• Do you know what a *ransom* is? Look it up and write the definition.

Yes, a ransom is a price that is paid so that something can be freed. Jesus paid the price of your sin so that you could be free. He died so that you would not have to die.

All you have to do is believe—and that is what we have been talking about throughout so many of our digs. He came to prove who He was so people would believe. And He came to die so that those who believe would not have to die.

Remember too that you discovered He came to be a servant. Think about how He served the men He loved when He washed their feet. Did you remember that we said we were going to see how He really served them? It is coming!

Jesus came to pay the price so that you can have eternal life. He came to be your ransom from sin!

Now I call that awesome beyond awesome! Incredible beyond incredible! Amazing beyond amazing! Someone loved you enough to die for you so that you could live! He paid a price for your sin! He wants you to have the gift of eternal life! All you have to do is believe!

Well, you have come to the end of an amazing dig! The next dig is our last. Hard to believe! But in it you will discover how Jesus serves all of mankind, how He glorifies the Father, how the Father glorifies Him, and what He did to be sure you would believe! All in one dig! So rest up and prepare to be amazed by what you will find—the greatest treasures know to man!

Truth Treasures for the Week

1.

2.

3.

Bury the Treasure:

I came that they might have life, and might have it abundantly (John 10:10).

Truth Trackers

The Time to Pray

We're learning so much about Jesus and His life as we study, aren't we! He always shows us the best way to live, doesn't He?

Think about what He did when He was faced with the most difficult thing in His life. What have we done at the start of every new dig? That's right! Jesus was always checking in with headquarters, too.

To learn more about prayer and when you should pray, follow the instructions below and look for the truths you find in the section below callen *Hidden Truths*.

Instructions:
1) God through each line of type below and cross out the following letters:

    B,J,Q,X,Z

    Go through once and cross out the Bs. Then go back and cross out the Js. Then the Qs, the Xs, and finally the Zs.
2) Now look at the letters left in number one and see what words you can form from the remaining letters. Write what you see, and discover a truth about prayer!
3) Do the same to number 2 and 3.

Hidden Truths

1. P B Q R A Y Q W Z X I T Q H B X O Z U B Z T C Q E A X S B I Q N X Z G

    Hidden Truth: _____

2. Q B X I S Z A B Q N X Y B O Q Q N B X E S U F B Q F E X R Z I B N G ?
   L X E Z Z T Q B H X Z I Q M B P Q R Z X A Q Y

    Hidden Truth: _____
    _____

3. B X W Q E Z P B Q X R Z A B Y F Q O B R Y Q Q O B U Z A L W X A Y B S

    Hidden Truth: _____

solution on page 198

Dig 12

The Greatest Victory of All

Tools of the Trade

1. Colored pencils
2. Pen or pencil
3. Dictionary
4. Jesus' Last Hours on pages 156-157
5. The Timeline of the Life of Christ on pages 191-192
6. The Last Three Days on page 185

Directions for Diggers

In this dig, you will uncover some of the treasures about Jesus' death. You will also discover that He died so that you could believe. You will find how He glorified His Father and how His Father glorified Him. And you will unearth the amazing treasure of what Jesus is doing today for you! At the end of this dig, you will have many treasures to add to your chest!

LAYER ONE: Torturing Jesus

Let's begin digging at the same place we ended last time so that you will not miss any of what we are searching for.

1. Read Matthew 27:26 to be reminded of how our last dig ended.

Truth Trackers: Jesus Our Savior and Friend

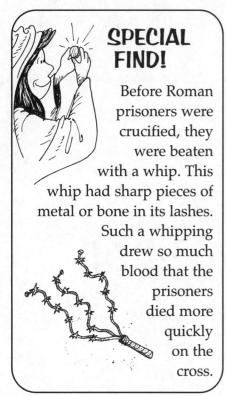

SPECIAL FIND!

Before Roman prisoners were crucified, they were beaten with a whip. This whip had sharp pieces of metal or bone in its lashes. Such a whipping drew so much blood that the prisoners died more quickly on the cross.

26Then he released Barabbas for them; but after having Jesus scourged, he handed Him over to be crucified.

Right. Now you remember, don't you? Jesus had been condemned to die on the cross because the crowed demanded that Pilate let a common criminal go free and crucify Jesus! And don't miss the fact that Pilate had Jesus scourged. That means that the soldiers whipped His back with a whip. It was called flogging.

2. Dig through the verses below to see what else the soldiers do with Jesus before they take Him away to be crucified.

27Then the soldiers of the governor took Jesus into the Praetorium and gathered the whole *Roman* cohort around Him. **28**They stripped Him and put a scarlet robe on Him. **29**And after twisting together a crown of thorns, they put it on His head, and a reed in His right hand; and they knelt down before Him and mocked Him, saying, "Hail, King of the Jews!" **30**They spat on Him, and took the reed and *began* to beat Him on the head. **31**After they had mocked Him, they took the *scarlet* robe off Him and put His *own* garments back on Him, and led Him away to crucify Him. **32**And as they were coming out, they found a man of Cryene named Simon, whom they pressed into service to bear His cross. **33**And when they had come to a place called Golgotha, which means Place of a Skull. (Matthew 27:27-33)

• Isn't it horrible to read about how cruel these men were to Jesus? And think too about the fact that He is the most powerful person on earth! He could have stopped them. But He didn't because it was all a part of God's plan! What do they do first to Jesus? Dig in verse 28.

• When you dig in verse 29, you discover that these men then made a crown for Jesus. What did they make it from?

• You also discover in verses 28-29 that these soldiers had put a purple robe on Jesus. Then they put a reed in Jesus' hand—like a scepter that a king carries. What do they do then?

The Greatest Victory of All

• Yes, they were making fun of Jesus for saying that He was the King of heaven. In verse 30, what happened?

• In verses 31-33, they take the robe off Jesus and put His clothes back on Him. Then they get ready to take Him to crucify Him. Criminals always had to carry their cross to the place were they were to be crucified. But we see that these men got someone to help Jesus. Many people think that they made this man help Him because they had beaten Him so badly that He was too weak to carry the cross. Who do they have help Jesus?

3. If you dig through all of the verses that Matthew, Mark, Luke, and John wrote about what happened on the day Jesus died, you will see that many people followed Him to the place where they were going to crucify Him. The place was called Golgatha or the Place of the Skull.

His mother was in the crowd too. Many of these people made fun of Him and mocked Him while He hung on the cross. Others were very, very sad that Jesus was being put to death.

And you will see in the verses below that Jesus was hung on a cross between two other men who were being crucified on that day. Both of these men were criminals.

Read these verses and see what Jesus said about those who crucified Him.

33 When they came to the place called The Skull, there they crucified Him and the criminals, one on the right and the other on the left. 34 But Jesus was saying, "Father, forgive them; for they do not know what they are doing." And they cast lots, dividing up His garments among themselves. 35 And the people stood by, looking on. And even the rulers were sneering at Him, saying, "He saved others; let Him save Himself if this is the Christ of God, His Chosen One." 36 The soldiers also mocked Him, coming up to Him, offering Him sour wine, 37 and saying, "If You are the King of the Jews, save Yourself!" (Luke 23:33-37)

• What does Jesus say to His Father in verse 34?

SPECIAL FIND!

The thorns that the soldiers used to make a crown for Jesus were very, very large and very, very strong.

When we think of thorns, we think of thorns from a rose bush. But these thorns were from a bush that grows in Israel that has thorns the size of a large nail!

Isn't it amazing that Jesus would pray for the people who were killing Him? But He knew that they had no idea He was the Son of God. They just did not believe.

You have done a lot of hard work today to come to this point, and I am proud of you. Take a moment and think about all you have discovered. And thank God today that He had a plan. And thank Jesus that He was willing to follow the plan all the way through to the end.

In the next dig, we will see some of the things that happen while Jesus hangs on the cross dying, and we will see who comes to bury Him when He is dead.

I hope you will think about all of the treasures you have uncovered and be very grateful for them. I will meet you in Layer Two.

LAYER TWO: Jesus Dies

Let's begin again with the crucifixion and see what treasures are waiting for us.

1. Jesus has been led to the place where He will be crucified, and He has prayed for those who are involved in putting Him to death. While He hung on the cross, people in the crowd made fun of Him, the soldiers gave Him sour wine to drink instead of water, some soldiers divided His clothes and bet on who would win them, even the chief priests of the Jews were saying cruel things. Then a very amazing thing happened!

44It was now about the sixth hour, and darkness fell over the whole land until the ninth hour, (Luke 23:44)

- What fell over the land?

The Greatest Victory of All

- What hour was it when the darkness fell?

- How long did the darkness last? Until what hour?

2. Dig in the verses to see what happened next at the ninth hour.

> **SPECIAL FIND!**
> The earth was dark for three hours as Jesus died. Think about one of the names He called Himself that had to do with light. Yes, "the light of the world." These men were killing Jesus, the light of the world, and all of a sudden it was very dark!

⁴⁶About the ninth hour Jesus cried out with a loud voice, saying, "ELI, ELI, LAMA SABACHTHANI?" that is, "MY GOD, MY GOD, WHY HAVE YOU FORSAKEN ME?" ⁴⁷And some of those who were standing there, when they heard it, *began* saying, "This man is calling for Elijah." ⁴⁸Immediately one of them ran, and taking a sponge, he filled it with sour wine and put it on a reed, and gave Him a drink. ⁴⁹But the rest *of them* said, "Let us see whether Elijah will come to save Him." ⁵⁰And Jesus cried out again with a loud voice, and yielded up His spirit. (Matthew 27:46-50)

- At the ninth hour, what does Jesus cry out?

Can you imagine that God would leave Jesus when He was dying? God did turn His face away in those last moments of Jesus' death because Jesus became sin for you and me as He died. Our sin killed Him. Remember that the price of sin is death, and Jesus paid it.

But God is a holy God, and He cannot look on sin. And Jesus became the sin of the entire world as He died!

- Jesus dies just after He cried out and became sin. What does verse 50 say about His death?

3. Even as Jesus died, someone believed! Let's see who. Write who it is below.

³⁹When the centurion, who was standing right in front of Him, saw the way He breathed His last, he said, "Truly this man was the Son of God!" (Mark 15:39)

- Yes, one of the soldiers who was at the cross! What did he say about Jesus?

Truth Trackers: *Jesus Our Savior and Friend*

4. Now, Jesus' body must be buried. Let's see who takes care of this the burial. I think you will recognize one of the men. See if you can. List their names below.

³⁸After these things Joseph of Arimathea, being a disciple of Jesus, but a secret *one* for fear of the Jews, asked Pilate that he might take away the body of Jesus; and Pilate granted permission. So he came and took away His body. ³⁹Nicodemus, who had first come to Him by night, also came, bringing a mixture of myrrh and aloes, about a hundred pounds *weight*. ⁴⁰So they took the body of Jesus and bound it in linen wrappings with the spices, as is the burial custom of the Jews. ⁴¹Now in the place where He was crucified there was a garden, and in the garden a new tomb in which no one had yet been laid. ⁴²Therefore because of the Jewish day of preparation, since the tomb was nearby, they laid Jesus there. (John 19:38-42)

SPECIAL FIND! Centurions were important Roman army soldiers who were officers. Each centurion commanded one hundred soldiers in the army. Centurions expected complete obedience from their men.

Do you remember Nicodemus? If you can't, go back to Layer One of Dig Four on pages 54-55 and refresh your memory. Now we know that he must have believed what Jesus told him!

• Who does verse 38 tell you that Joseph was?

• Where is the tomb they put Jesus in?

5. Let's see what Mark tells us about the burial that John didn't.

⁴⁶Joseph bought a linen cloth, took Him down, wrapped Him in the linen cloth and laid Him in a tomb which had been hewn out in the rock; and he rolled a stone against the entrance of the tomb. (Mark 15:46)

• What was done after Jesus was put in the tomb?

6. Turn to the Timeline of the Life of Christ on pages 191-192 and mark the two events you have uncovered today.

The Greatest Victory of All

Well, it was a very, very sad day for those who loved Jesus and believed Him. But it was a day that heaven rejoiced because Jesus had glorified His Father! How? He had obeyed what they had agreed to do to pay for mankind's sin. Even though Jesus in His last hours asked if there was any other way, He did not back out. He went all the way for you and all people!

And although He had told His men that He would rise from the dead in three days, I am sure it would be hard to believe after watching Him be treated so badly and crucified. But...they had seen Him raise Lazarus!

7. Turn to Jesus' Last Hours on pages 156-157. Find the sketch of the crucifixion and color it.

Take a good break and get ready for a super exciting time of digging in Layer Three! Good news is just around the corner! Now God is about to glorify the Son, Jesus!

LAYER THREE:

You are about to dig out one of the most fantastic treasures of all the Bible! I can't wait, so let's go!

1. This section is a little long, but is so exciting I don't think you will even notice how long it takes to dig through it!

¹When the Sabbath was over, Mary Magdalene, and Mary the *mother* of James, and Salome, bought spices, so that they might come and anoint Him. ²Very early on the first day of the week, they came˙ to the tomb when the sun had risen. ³They were saying to one another, "Who will roll away the stone for us from the entrance of the tomb?" ⁴Looking up, they saw˙ that the stone had been rolled away, although it was extremely large. ⁵Entering the tomb, they saw a young man sitting at the right, wearing a white robe; and they were amazed. ⁶And he said˙ to them, "Do not be amazed; you are looking for Jesus the Nazarene, who has been crucified. He has risen; He is not here; behold, *here is* the place where they laid Him. ⁷"But go, tell His disciples and Peter, 'He is going ahead of you to Galilee; there you will see Him, just as He told you.'" ⁸They went out and fled from the tomb, for trembling and astonishment had gripped them; and they said nothing to anyone, for they were afraid. ⁹Now after He had risen early on the first day of the week, He first appeared to Mary Magdalene, from whom He had cast out seven demons. ¹⁰She went and reported to those who had been with Him,

while they were mourning and weeping. **11**When they heard that He was alive and had been seen by her, they refused to believe it. **12**After that, He appeared in a different form to two of them while they were walking along on their way to the country. **13**They went away and reported it to the others, but they did not believe them either.
14Afterward He appeared to the eleven themselves as they were reclining at the table; and He reproached them for their unbelief and hardness of heart, because they had not believed those who had seen Him after He had risen. (Mark 16:1-14)

• Some of Jesus' friends were going back to His tomb to take more spices to put on His body. Just like people today go back to graves to take flowers. They were wondering how they would be able to move the large stone that sealed the tomb. But an amazing thing happened. What was it? Dig in verse 4 to see.

• In verse 5 you saw who was in the tomb. Who was it? And what does he tell Jesus' friends about where Jesus is?

• Then what does this young man tell them to say to Peter and the disciples? (By the way, Matthew and John both call this young man an angel!)

• How do the friends respond in verse 8?

• But we see that Jesus Himself appears then to several people. He first appears to Mary Magdalene. She then goes to the others who had been with Him—His disciples. What does verse 11 say about how they responded?

• Next Jesus appears to two men who had been with Him, and they tell others. These others do not believe either. It must have been confusing! But then in verse 14, whom do we see that Jesus appeared to?

Yes, He goes to the 11 men who had been with Him from the beginning of His ministry! And He tells them something very special that we will uncover in our next layer!

The Greatest Victory of All

2. Let's dig through two more verses to find a treasure that is a sad truth, but it is a rewarding find.

11Now while they were on their way, some of the guard came into the city and reported to the chief priests all that had happened. **12**And when they had assembled with the elders and consulted together, they gave a large sum of money to the soldiers, **13**and said, "You are to say, 'His disciples came by night and stole Him away while we were asleep.' **14**"And if this should come to the governor's ears, we will win him over and keep you out of trouble." **15**And they took the money and did as they had been instructed; and this story was widely spread among the Jews, *and is* to this day. (Matthew 28:11-15)

• When the guards who were at the tomb come to the city and tell the chief priests (the Jewish religious leaders) what has happened, they get a group together to discuss this turn of events. What do they give to the soldiers and what do they tell them to do?

• What do the soldiers do?

• How long has this story been told?

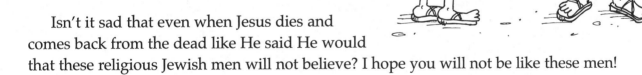

Isn't it sad that even when Jesus dies and comes back from the dead like He said He would that these religious Jewish men will not believe? I hope you will not be like these men!

3. Turn to the Timeline of the Life of Christ on pages 191-192 and mark this amazing, awesome event!

4. Also, color the sketch of the resurrection on Jesus' Last Hours on pages 156-157.
JESUS IS ALIVE! How exciting! He died for you and all mankind, and then after three days He rose from the dead! This is what He did so that you would believe! He came back from the dead. He beat death because He paid the price for sin. And in raising Jesus from the dead, God glorified His Son.

By raising Jesus from the dead, God was saying that all that Jesus did was enough! He was saying that Jesus paid the price and that He was satisfied!

Because the price for sin has been paid, you can be free! You only must believe!

Truth Trackers: *Jesus Our Savior and Friend*

What a dig! What treasures! They are the things that lead to eternal life! Hold on to them and study them hard! I will see you in Layer Four soon.

LAYER FOUR: Now It's Our Turn

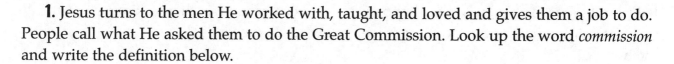

Let's continue digging in Mark's story of Jesus' resurrection! I know you must be excited to see what happened next!

¹⁵And He said to them, "Go into all the world and preach the gospel to all creation. (Mark 16:15)

1. Jesus turns to the men He worked with, taught, and loved and gives them a job to do. People call what He asked them to do the Great Commission. Look up the word *commission* and write the definition below.

• Where does Jesus tell these men to go?

• What does He tell them to do?

Yes, He tells them to go to the world and spread the news about Him—that He came and proved He was God's Son and then He died and rose from the dead to pay the price for sin!

2. Do you think these men did what Jesus asked them to do? Read Mark 16: 20 below to see.

²⁰And they went out and preached everywhere, while the Lord worked with them, and confirmed the word by the signs that followed.

- Where did they preach?

Isn't it awesome that Mark tells us the Lord worked with them. Even though He could not be with them daily, He helped them. Remember about the Holy Spirit!

Let's dig out one more incredible treasure! Look again and see what confirmed the word they were telling people. *Confirmed* means that it showed that what they were saying was true. What did the Lord use to confirm the word they were teaching?

Don't you think that is cool? The very thing that God used to show people Jesus was His Son is what Jesus uses to show people that these men are telling the truth about Him! Signs! Think again about some of the signs Jesus did. Can you record just two?

3. Turn again to the Timeline of the Life of Christ on pages 191-192 and mark the event you uncovered today.

It is so neat to think that Jesus didn't just disappear, isn't it? He told these men what to do! And He helped them do it! He will tell you what to do too. He will never leave you wondering. He will always be trustworthy and show you the correct way! And He will help you do it! Super amazing!

I cannot believe that the next layer is the last layer of our time together! You will have to sign up for another dig soon! See you in Layer Five!

LAYER FIVE: Jesus Goes Home

Today you will discover what Jesus did after He rose from the dead—and it is what He is doing this very day! Awesome!

1. Read Mark 16:19 and discover what Jesus did after He gave these men the Great Commission.

19So then, when the Lord Jesus had spoken to them, He was received up into heaven and sat down at the right hand of God.

• Where does Jesus go?

• What does He do when He gets there?

2. Let's dig in one other verse that tells us what He did in a different way. Read Hebrews 1:3 and think hard as you read.

3And He is the radiance of His glory and the exact representation of His nature, and upholds all things by the word of His power. When He had made purification of sins, He sat down at the right hand of the Majesty on high…

• What does it tell you that Jesus did?

• But when did He do it? What did He do before He sat down? This verse uses big words, but it is a great treasure!

Hope you found it. It says "when He made purification of sins." Do you know what *purify* means? Yes, to clean. So this verse says that after Jesus cleaned up our sin, He sat down!
Isn't that great! Just what we have been discovering—just in bigger words!

3. Think back to Dig Ten and see if you can remember one of the things Jesus tells the men who are so special to Him about what He is going to do for them. It has to do with the future. If you can't remember look back to Layer Four on page 151.
Yes, He says He is going to prepare a place for them to come. And this is a part of what Jesus is doing in heaven now! Jesus is preparing a place for these men He loved, and He is preparing a place for YOU if you believe in Him!

The Greatest Victory of All

4. One other verse we can dig in will help you understand what Jesus is doing for you today.

^{25}Therefore He is able also to save forever those who draw near to God through Him, since He always lives to make intercession for them. (Hebrews 7:25)

• What does this verse say Jesus is able to do?

Yes, He saves those who draw near to God! And do you remember that we dug out a treasure that showed us that while Jesus was on earth, God drew men to Him? What a partnership!

• What does Jesus live to do?

Intercession means that He is praying. He lives to pray for them!
Read the verse again and think about whom the word *them* is talking about. I think it is talking about those people whom He saves. So if you are saved, if you have believed in Jesus, He is praying for you!
Now that amazes me! To think that this very day Jesus is praying for you! You must be very, very excited—even beyond excited to think that the most powerful person who ever lived on earth now lives in heaven and part of His job is to pray for you!
Too awesome! Too incredible! Too amazing! Too super! But sooooo true!

4. One last time, turn to the Timeline of the Life of Christ on pages 191-192 and mark this last event you discovered!

Well, we have come to the end of an astounding dig. I trust you will treasure all the gems you uncovered and that you will not waste them! I hope you will use them to be all that Jesus wants you to be!

And I really look forward to digging with you again soon in another dig!

Truth Trackers: Jesus Our Savior and Friend

Truth Treasures for the Week

1.

2.

3.

Bury the Treasure:

He who has the Son has life; he who does not have the Son of God does not have the life (1 John 5:12).

The Last Three Days

When Jesus was preparing to die, He prayed, "Not My will, but Thine be done." As you work through this crossword puzzle, be thinking about the great sacrifice that Jesus made for you and me so that we could have LIFE! Find a place for each word in the squares below.

Across

1. Jesus died so you could have this eternally
5. What Jesus did in Gethsemane
6. The city where Jesus was crucified
7. The Garden where Jesus prayed
8. Jesus had one made of thorns
9. A soldier pierced Jesus' side with one
11. What Jesus was buried in
12. Herod was a ruler from Rome, so he was called a _____
13. The ruler who became Pilate's friend during Jesus' trial

Down

2. Jesus prayed to Him
3. The soldiers put a purple one on Jesus
4. Jesus died on one
6. Group of people who were upset by Jesus' miracles and who wanted to crucify Him
7. Jesus' tomb was in one called Gethsemane
10. This was the penalty for sin
11. Jesus had a crown made of these
12. Herod's job was to do this

solution on page 199

Treasure Map

Matthew 1:18–2:23

- Chapter 1 -

¹⁸Now the birth of Jesus Christ was as follows: when His mother Mary had been betrothed to Joseph, before they came together she was found to be with child by the Holy Spirit. ¹⁹And Joseph her husband, being a righteous man and not wanting to disgrace her, planned to send her away secretly. ²⁰But when he had considered this, behold, an angel of the Lord appeared to him in a dream, saying, "Joseph, son of David, do not be afraid to take Mary as your wife; for the Child who has been conceived in her is of the Holy Spirit. ²¹"She will bear a Son; and you shall call His name Jesus, for He will save His people from their sins." ²²Now all this took place to fulfill what was spoken by the Lord through the prophet: ²³"BEHOLD, THE VIRGIN SHALL BE WITH CHILD AND SHALL BEAR A SON, AND THEY SHALL CALL HIS NAME IMMANUEL," which translated means, "GOD WITH US." ²⁴And Joseph arose from his sleep, and sis as the angel of the Lord commanded him, and took *her* as his wife, ²⁵and kept her a virgin until she gave birth to a Son; and he called His name Jesus.

- Chapter 2 -

¹Now after Jesus was born in Bethlehem in Judea in the days of Herod the king, behold, magi from the east arrived in Jerusalem, saying ²"Where is He who has been born King of the Jews? For we saw His star in the east, and have come to worship Him." ³And when Herod the king heard it, he was troubled, and all Jerusalem with him. ⁴And gathering together all the chief priests and scribes of the people, he *began* to inquire of them where the Christ was to be born. ⁵And they said to him, "In Bethlehem of Judea, for so it has been written by the prophet,

⁶AND YOU, BETHLEHEM, LAND OF JUDAH,
ARE BY NO MEANS LEAST AMONG THE LEADERS OF JUDAH;
FOR OUT OF YOU SHALL COME FORTH A RULER,
WHO WILL SHEPHERD MY PEOPLE ISRAEL.'"

⁷Then Herod secretly called the magi, and ascertained from them the time the star appeared. ⁸And he sent them to Bethlehem, and said, "Go and make careful search for the Child; and when you have found *Him*, report to me, that I too may come and worship Him." ⁹And having heard the king, they went their way; and lo, the star,

which they had seen in the east, went on before them, until it came and stood over where the Child was. **10**And when they saw the star, they rejoiced exceedingly with great joy. **11**And they came into the house and saw the Child with Mary His mother; and they fell down and worshiped Him; and opening their treasures they presented to Him gifts of gold and frankincense and myrrh. **12**And having been warned *by* God in a dream not to return to Herod, they departed for their own country by another way.

13Now when they had gone, behold, an angel of the Lord appeared˙ to Joseph in a dream and said, "Get up! Take the Child and His mother and flee to Egypt, and remain there until I tell you; for Herod is going to search for the Child to destroy Him."
14So Joseph got up and took the Child and His mother while it was still night, and left for Egypt. **15**He remained there until the death of Herod. *This was* to fulfill what had been spoken by the Lord through the prophet: "Out of Egypt I called My Son."
16Then when Herod saw that he had been tricked by the magi, he became very enraged, and sent and slew all the male children who were in Bethlehem and all its vicinity, from two years old and under, according to the time which he had determined from the magi.

19But when Herod died, behold, an angel of the Lord appeared˙ in a dream to Joseph in Egypt, and said, **20**"Get up, take the Child and His mother, and go into the land of Israel; for those who sought the Child's life are dead." **21**So Joseph got up, took the Child and His mother, and came into the land of Israel. **22**But when he heard that Archelaus was reigning over Judea in place of his father Herod, he was afraid to go there. Then after being warned *by God* in a dream, he left for the regions of Galilee, **23**and came and lived in a city called Nazareth. *This was* to fulfill what was spoken through the prophets: "He shall be called a Nazarene."

Luke 1:26-35; 2:1-39

- Chapter 1 -

26Now in the sixth month the angel Gabriel was sent from God to a city in Galilee called Nazareth, **27**to a virgin engaged to a man whose name was Joseph, of the descendants of David; and the virgin's name was Mary. **28**And coming in, he said to her, "Greetings, favored one! The Lord *is* with you." **29**But she was very perplexed at *this* statement, and kept pondering what kind of salutation this was. **30**The angel said to her, "Do not be afraid, Mary; for you have found favor with God. **31**"And behold, you will conceive in your womb and bear a son, and you shall name Him Jesus. **32**"He will be great and will be called the Son of the Most High; and the Lord God will give Him the throne of His father David; **33**and He will reign over the house of Jacob forever, and His kingdom will have no end." **34**Mary said to the angel, "How can this be, since I am a virgin?" **35**The angel answered and said to her, "The Holy Spirit will come upon you, and the power of the Most High will overshadow you; and for that reason the holy Child shall be called the Son of God."

- Chapter 2 -

1Now it came about in those days that a decree went out from Caesar Augustus, that a census be taken of all the inhabited earth. **2**This was the first census taken while Quirinius was governor of Syria. **3**And all were proceeding to register for the census, everyone to his own city. **4**And Joseph also went up from Galilee, from the city of Nazareth, to Judea, to the city of David, which is called Bethlehem, because he was of the house and family of David, **5**in order to register along with Mary, who was engaged to him, and was with child. **6**And it came about that while they were there, the days were completed for her to give birth. **7**And she gave birth to her first-born son; and she wrapped Him in cloths, and laid Him in a manger, because there was no room for them in the inn. **8**And in the same region there were *some* shepherds staying out in the fields, and keeping watch over their flock by night. **9**And an angel of the Lord suddenly stood before them, and the glory of the Lord shone around them; and they were terribly frightened. **10**And the angel said to them, "Do not be afraid; for behold, I bring you good news of a great joy which shall be for all the people; **11**for today in the city of David there has been born for you a Savior, who is Christ the Lord. **12**"And this *will be* a sign for you: you will find a baby wrapped in cloths, and lying in a manger." **13**And suddenly there appeared with the angel a multitude of the heavenly host praising God, and saying,

14"Glory to God in the highest,
And on earth peace among men with whom He is pleased."

15And it came about when the angels had gone away from them into heaven, that the shepherds *began* saying to one another, "Let us go straight to Bethlehem then, and see this thing that has happened which the Lord has made known to us." **16**And they came in haste and found their way to Mary and Joseph, and the baby as He lay in the manger. **17**And when they had seen this, they made known the statement which had been told them about this Child. **18**And all who heard it wondered at the things which were told them by the shepherds. **19**But Mary treasured up all these things, pondering them in her heart. **20**And the shepherds went back, glorifying and praising God for all that they had heard and seen, just as had been told them. **21**And when eight days were completed before His circumcision, His name was *then* called Jesus, the name given by the angel before He was conceived in the womb. **22**And when the days for their purification according to the law of Moses were completed, they brought Him up to Jerusalem to present Him to the Lord **23**(as it is written in the Law of the Lord, "EVERY FIRST-BORN MALE THAT OPENS THE WOMB SHALL BE CALLED HOLY TO THE LORD"), **24**and to offer a sacrifice according to what was said in the Law of the Lord, "A PAIR OF TURTLEDOVES, OR TWO YOUNG PIGEONS."**25**And behold, there was a man in Jerusalem whose name was Simeon; and this man was righteous and devout, looking for the consolation of Israel; and the Holy Spirit was upon him. **26**And it had been revealed to him by the Holy Spirit that he would not see death before he had seen the Lord's Christ. **27**And he came in the Spirit into the temple; and when the parents brought in the child Jesus, to carry out for Him the custom of the Law, **28**then he took Him into his arms, and blessed God, and said,

29"Now Lord, Thou dost let Thy bond-servant depart
In peace, according to Thy word;
30For my eyes have seen Thy salvation,
31Which Thou hast prepared in the presence of all peoples,
32A LIGHT OF REVELATION TO THE GENTILES,
And the glory of Thy people Israel."

33And His father and mother were amazed at the things which were being said about Him. 34And Simeon blessed them, and said to Mary His mother, "Behold, this *Child* is appointed for the fall and rise of many in Israel, and for a sign to be opposed— 35and a sword will pierce even your own soul—to the end that thoughts from many hearts may be revealed." 36And there was a prophetess, Anna the daughter of Phanuel, of the tribe of Asher. She was advanced in years, having lived with a husband seven years after her marriage, 37and then as a widow to the age of eighty-four. And she never left the temple, serving night and day with fastings and prayers. 38And at that very moment she came up and *began* giving thanks to God, and continued to speak of Him to all those who were looking for the redemption of Jerusalem. 39And when they had performed everything according to the Law of the Lord, they returned to Galilee, to their own city of Nazareth. (Luke 2:1-39)

John 1:1-17

1In the beginning was the Word, and the Word was with God, and the Word was God. 2He was in the beginning with God. 3All things came into being through Him, and apart from Him nothing came into being that has come into being. 4In Him was life, and the life was the Light of men. 5The Light shines in the darkness, and the darkness did not comprehend it.
6There came a man sent from God, whose name was John. 7He came as a witness, to testify about the Light, so that all might believe through him. 8He was not the Light, but *he came* to testify about the Light.
9There was the true Light which, coming into the world, enlightens every man. 10He was in the world, and the world was made through Him, and the world did not know Him. 11He came to His own, and those who were His own did not receive Him. 12But as many as received Him, to them He gave the right to become children of God, *even* to those who believe in His name, 13who were born, not of blood nor of the will of the flesh nor of the will of man, but of God.
14And the Word became flesh, and dwelt among us, and we saw His glory, glory as of the only begotten from the Father, full of grace and truth. 15John testified* about Him and cried out, saying, "This was He of whom I said, 'He who comes after me has a higher rank than I, for He existed before me.'" 16For of His fullness we have all received, and grace upon grace. 17For the Law was given through Moses; grace and truth were realized through Jesus Christ. (John 1:1-17)

Timeline of the Life of Christ

There are four books in the Bible that tell us about Jesus' life. These books are called the Gospels. They were each written by a different man. Many of the things Jesus did are recorded in more than one of the Gospels. But some things about Him and some of the things He did are talked about in only one or two of the Gospels.

Matthew, who was one of Jesus' twelve apostles, wrote the Gospel of Matthew. His goal was to show the Jewish people that Jesus was the Messiah who had been talked about in the Old Testament. He wanted Jesus' own people to see who He was.

Mark was a young man who wrote down many of the stories that Peter told about Jesus. Mark's goal was to be sure that everyone knew who Jesus was, so he told lots of the things that Jesus did while He was on earth.

Luke was a doctor! He traveled with the apostle Paul after Jesus died. Luke wrote his gospel so that there would be a record of things *as* they happened. He told us that he was writing the things Jesus did in the order they happened! He wanted there to be a chronological record of the events of Jesus' life. (Remember, though, that Luke did not record everything that Jesus said and did. The Bible isn't big enough for that!)

John also was one of the 12 men Jesus asked to work with Him and spend time with Him. His goal in writing his gospel was to record some of the miracles and signs that Jesus did—the ones that he thought would help people believe that Jesus was who He said He was! He, too, wanted to be sure that people believed in the Son of God.

On the next page is a simple timeline that will help you see the order of the events that we will cover in our dig. You will be reminded as we go to check off these events as you uncover them. You can write in the number of the dig in the blank when you discover the event. I think this practice may help you remember what you discover.

Truth Trackers: Jesus Our Savior and Friend

Timeline

Studied	Event	Place	Bible Verse
Dig _____	**Jesus Is born**	Bethlehem	Luke 2:1-20
Dig _____	**Jesus Goes to the Temple**	Jerusalem	Luke 2:41-52
Dig _____	**Jesus Is Baptized**	Jordan River	Luke 3:21-23a
Dig _____	**Jesus Is Tempted by Satan**	The Desert	Luke 4:1-13
Dig _____	**Jesus Chooses His Disciples**	Galilee	Mark 3:13-19
Dig _____	**Jesus Performs His First Miracle**	Cana	John 2:1-11
Dig _____	**Jesus Heals Official's Son**	Cana	John 4:46-54
Dig _____	**Jesus Heals Man Lame for 38 Years**	Jerusalem	John 5:1-13
Dig _____	**Jesus Feeds 5,000**	Bethsaida	John 6:1-14
Dig _____	**Jesus Walks on the Water**	Sea of Galilee	John 6:16-21
Dig _____	**Jesus Heals Man Blind from Birth**	Jerusalem	John 9:1-17
Dig _____	**Jesus Raises Lazarus from the Dead**	Bethany	John 11:1-47
Dig _____	**Jesus Eats the Last Supper**	Jerusalem	John 13-17
Dig _____	**Jesus Prays in Gethsemane**	Jerusalem	Matthew 26:36-46
Dig _____	**Jesus Is Arrested**	Jerusalem	John 18:2-5
Dig _____	**Jesus Is Crucified**	Jerusalem	Matthew 27:27-56
Dig _____	**Jesus Is Buried**	Jerusalem	John 19:38-42
Dig _____	**Jesus Is Raised from the Dead**	Jerusalem	Mark 16:1-8
Dig _____	**Jesus Appears to the Disciples**	Jerusalem	Mark 16:15
Dig _____	**Jesus Goes to Heaven**	Mount of Olives	Mark 16:17

Key to Games

Maze to the Manger

found on page 20

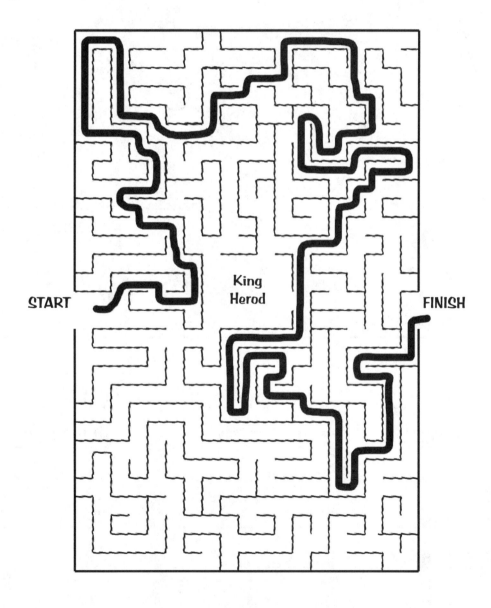

Truth Trackers: Jesus Our Savior and Friend

Before and After Jesus Saves You

found on page 33

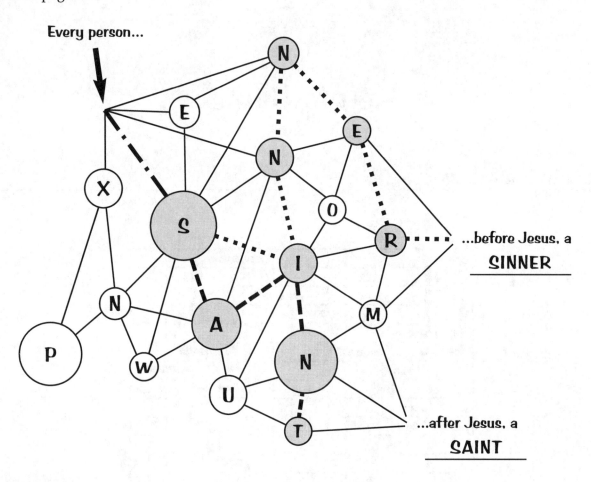

...before Jesus, a SINNER

...after Jesus, a SAINT

A Puzzle of People and Places

found on page 52

1. **TEMPLE**
2. **SEA OF GALILEE**
3. **MARY**
4. **JOSEPH**
5. **NAZARETH**
6. **CAPERNAUM**
7. **BETHLEHEM**
8. **SYNAGOGUE**
9. **HEROD**
10. **GOD**
11. **EGYPT**
12. **SHEPHERDS**
13. **JOHN**
14. **ANGELS**

Key to Games

Name That Disciple!

found on page 67

Scrambled Name	Unscrambled Name
1. HOJN	J O H N̲₃
2. SEAMJ	J A̲₁₇ M E S̲₂
3. ERTEP	P̲₁₃ E T E R̲₉
4. WREDAN	A N̲₁₅ D R E W̲₄
5. PIHLIP	P H I L I̲₁₂ P
6. WEMLOOHTRAB	B̲₅ A R T H O̲₆ L O M E W̲₁₄
7. TTHEWAM	M A T T H E W̲₇
8. HOMAST	T H̲₈ O M A S̲₁₈
9. SMEAJ	J̲₁₆ A M E S̲₁₀
10. ASDUJ	J U D A S
11. DAEUSADHT	T H̲₁₁ A D D E A U S̲₁₉
12. MONIS	S̲₂₀ I̲₁ M O N

M E N̲   W H O   W O R S H I P E D   J E S U S
1 2 3   4 5 6   7 8 9 10 11 12 13 14 15   16 17 18 19 20

Key Words

found on page 84

1. L̲IGHT
2. CO̲IN
3. S̲HEEP
4. REPENT̲
5. F̲ATHER
6. CLAYTON̲
7. D̲IG
8. F̲OLLOWER
9. S̲ON
10. BU̲ILD
11. SINN̲ER
12. SAND̲

1	2	3	4	5	6	7	8	9	10	11	12
L	O	S	T	A	N	D	F	O	U	N	D

Connect the Dots to Truth

found on page 98

Love the Lord your God...

with all your

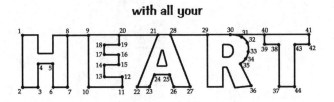

with all your

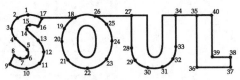

with all your

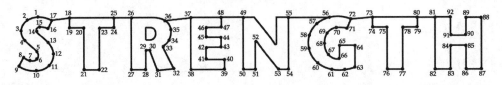

with all your

The Secret of Miracles

found on page 112

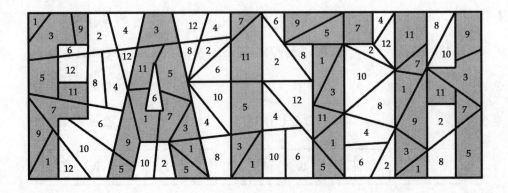

Key to Games

Decode the True Message of the Miracles

found on page 130

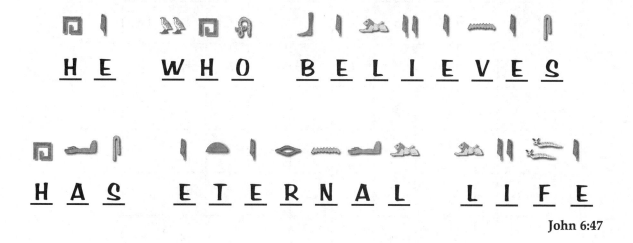

HE WHO BELIEVES
HAS ETERNAL LIFE

John 6:47

Name Hunt

found on page 141

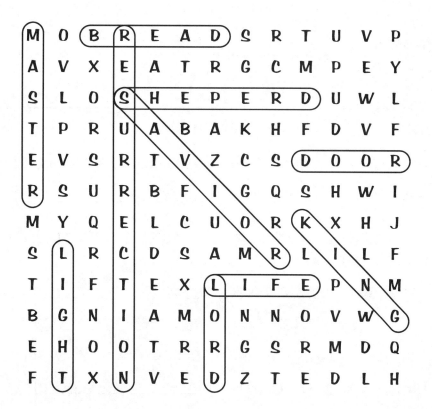

197

Truth Trackers: Jesus Our Savior and Friend

An Alphanumber Promise

found on page 158

9	27	23	9	12	12	27	3	15	13	5
I	W	I	L	L		C	O	M	E	
27	1	7	1	9	14	27	1	14	4	27
	A	G	A	I	N		A	N	D	
18	5	3	5	9	22	5	27	25	15	21
R	E	C	E	I	V	E		Y	O	U
27	20	15	27	13	25	19	5	12	6	27
	T	O		M	Y	S	E	L	F,	
20	8	1	20	27	23	8	5	18	5	27
T	H	A	T		W	H	E	R	E	
9	27	1	13	27	20	8	5	18	5	27
I		A	M,		T	H	E	R	E	
25	15	21	27	13	1	25	27	2	5	27
Y	O	U		M	A	Y		B	E	
1	12	19	15	27	10	15	8	14		
A	L	S	O.		J	O	H	N	14:3b	

The Time to Pray

found on page 170

Hidden Truths

1. P~~BQ~~RAY~~QWZXI~~T~~QHBXOZUBZTCQEAXSBIQNXZ~~G

   Hidden Truth: <u>PRAY WITHOUT CEASING</u>

2. ~~QBX~~IS ~~ZABQNXY~~ ~~BOQQNBXE~~SUF~~BQFEXRZI~~NG?
   L~~XEZZTQBHXZIQM~~ ~~BPQRZXAQ~~Y

   Hidden Truth: <u>IS ANYONE SUFFERING?</u>
   <u>LET HIM PRAY</u>

3. ~~BXWQEZP~~~~BQXRZA~~Y F~~QO~~R Y~~QQO~~~~BUZ~~AL~~WX~~AY~~BS~~

   Hidden Truth: <u>WE PRAY FOR YOU ALWAYS</u>

Now, remember to practice these hidden truths every day!

The Last Three Days

found on page 185

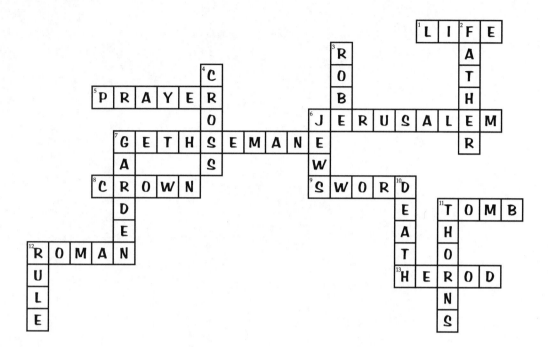